ALAS, IRAQ

RONALD RUNGE

iUniverse, Inc.
New York   Bloomington

Alas, Iraq

iUniverse books may be ordered through booksellers or by contacting:

iUniverse
1663 Liberty Drive
Bloomington, IN 47403
www.iuniverse.com
1-800-Authors (1-800-288-4677)

Because of the dynamic nature of the Internet, any Web addresses or links contained in this book may have changed since publication and may no longer be valid. The views expressed in this work are solely those of the author and do not necessarily reflect the views of the publisher, and the publisher hereby disclaims any responsibility for them.

ISBN: 978-1-4401-1471-7 (sc)
ISBN: 978-1-4401-1472-4 (ebook)

Printed in the United States of America

iUniverse rev. date: 12/30/08

Chapter I -
Sergeant "Bis"

The unyielding glare of Iraq's Diyala Province's sun, struck Sergeant First Class, Ian von Bismarck, better known to the other eight men of the Rifle Squad he commanded, forming part of the Seventh Squadron, Seventh Stryker Cavalry Regiment, Seven hundred eleventh Stryker Brigade, as Sergeant Bis, directly in the eyes.

Sergeant Bis was following his US Army Rifle Squad down the lowered ramp, and out of the back of their transport, the newest, most agile armored combat vehicle in Iraq, which they labeled the "Stryker".

The Stryker, also with a reputation as the most lethal, and best protected, of the US Army's combat vehicles, gave Sergeant Bis a confident assurance that it would provide the needed protection for his men, as his Rifle Squad quickly hit the now quiet, streets of this small Iraqi town, sitting on the east side of Diyala Province's bread basket, only a few miles west of Baghdad. As the Sergeant was ordered to do, he began a house to house search, looking for al-Qaeda irregulars, reported to be in the area.

Even though the temperature hovered in the upper nineties, and Bis, and his men, were clad in heavy combat boots, and clothing, including helmets, and bulletproof vests, Sergeant Bis watched extremely carefully, as his men, ignoring the heat, moved methodically, to and from each joined together, colorfully painted, cement block based housing units, busting down some of the mostly metal doors, if no one residing therein would quickly admit them after due notice.

Sergeant Bis, when that happened, would designate one of his men to blast open the door with a ten foot, six by six timber, which the squad carried with it, usually causing the door to spring open. Two of his squad men, stationed on each side, would then rush through the doorway, into the house, their automatic rifles ready to fire. This was to secure the inside, and it was followed up by two other squad riflemen. The rest of the squad would remain on guard outside the searched house.

A two hour search, covering two Iraqi city blocks, did not yield any al-Qaeda, but it did bring out several Iraqi's boasting of being Shi'ite Moslems in a Sunni area. They were herded out on to the street, where Sergeant Bis ordered them searched.

Bis watched, and then directed his corporal, John Ballard, "Search two of them at a time. Have them put their hands in back of their neck and lean their heads forward. Put two men on guard on each side, looking both ways, with their rifles ready to fire. Direct the two other squad men to hand and leg check each suspect for any weapons or al-Qaeda materials, including a thorough body pat down and search."

At the end of these three searching, heat filled hours, Sergeant Bis deciding that only one suspect merited further attention, told Corporal Ballard, "Handcuff him. Take him back to our Stryker. We will turn him over to the Captain, and he can worry about him," adding, "I can already see two or three other Stryker Units that deployed with us have returned."

"Let's get out of here," Corporal Ballard agreed. "It is spooky."

Bis's Squad marched the prisoner back to their combat vehicle, turned the captive over to the Captain, watched as the ramp was lowered, and reentered the Stryker. Hot as it was, they tried to relax, but the Sergeant told them, "Keep your helmets and vests on," adding, "And keep your rifle at the ready. We are not out of this yet."

For the first time, in the low key, but yet high key, three hour search, Sergeant Bis, after resuming his sergeant's seat in the front of the Stryker, felt a degree better, that things would now go alright, and let some of the extreme tenseness go out of his body.

The thirty-three-year-old Iowa native allowed himself to lean back a little in his seat, thinking, *"Thank God, and thank some thinking general in the US Army, for somehow getting my squad this Stryker. It is fast, and it is mobile. It can bring a lot of army infantry men into a firefight quickly, on Baghdad's deadly streets. It can, by using only twenty Strykers,*

deploy one hundred and twenty dismounted riflemen,
in less than an hour, anywhere in Baghdad, whereas
it would take forty armored Humvees, along with their
need for an additional eighty Humvee crewmen, just to
transport the Humvees and that number of troops."

Sergeant Bis continued thinking, *"The Iraqi
Sunni's militia, the Iraqi Shi'ite's militia, and the al-
Qaeda terrorists operating in Iraq, all using deadly, but
mostly hit and run tactics, and all of them ready and
willing to attack and kill the hated American soldier
whenever they have a chance, can only be countered by
being able to quickly bring a large number of boots into
the fight. With our Strykers, we are able to do that."*

The Sergeant smiled, thinking, *"This is my third
tour in Iraq, and being part of this Stryker Brigade,
is best in some twenty-three months of the toughest
combat in Iraq. The presence of this vehicle has been
a God-send for me, and for the US Army.*

*"In most Iraqi firefights I remember, around Mosul,
Talafar, al Kut, Baghdad, Baqubuh, and Najaf, there
has been only a handful of the usual enemy militia
rocket propelled grenades, able to penetrate a Stryker,"*
he thought. *"Although there have been several hundred,
or even several thousand, which have been fired at the
vehicle, though the majority of them probably struck
some part of the Stryker, most of them came through all
those fights without really significant damage,"* adding
more to his thoughts, *"As a matter of fact, the big killer
is the militia's roadside bombs, which, when full of
enough explosives, can destroy the best of the army's
armored Humvees, or even the MIA-2 tanks. However,
the blast resistant design of the Stryker, in both its*

wheel wells, and its bottom, has kept its riflemen mostly protected, compared to the others."

Getting ready to leave, the officer in charge of the operation, had gathered together all his deployed Stryker units. Bis felt his Stryker chariot start moving, and looking out his peek holes, saw his Stryker unit was situated in the middle of the line of eight Strykers, proceeding at a fast pace back toward their forward operating base located on the western edge of Baghdad. His unit would have to deploy out of that temporary base, for only another two days, and then be returned back to their Baghdad Green Zone, their permanent barracks for some well deserved rest and relaxation.

"Remember that two hundred fifty mile ride in a Stryker at sixty miles per hour, from Mosul to Baghdad, a few weeks ago?" Bis challenged his corporal, John Ballard, to recall.

"I hope we can get up to that speed," the corporal responded. "I don't like this place," adding, "At least, this time, we don't have to deal with the Sadrist's Mahdi Army in Sadr City. I talked to the guy's that had been deployed over there last week, and they told me, over half of the al-Maliki Iraqi Army and police force who were assigned there, defected to the Sadrs. They did not know who was a friend and who was foe. Scary."

Sergeant Bis nodded his heavy helmet in agreement, noting, "They follow the dictates of Sheik al Sadr, rather than any orders given them by al-Maliki's so called, Iraqi government," adding, "Sadr is mad at Maliki for abetting Bush's instructions to the Iraqi American generals, to suck it up 'to the old

Saddam Hussein's Sunnis. Bush, and the generals, wants to get an agreement to reestablish their long, vicious fight against the Saudi Sunni al-Qaeda, now operating in Iraq.'"

"The Iraqi Sunnis have already dispatched some of their suicide bombers against Iraqi al-Qaeda strongholds," the corporal interposed, "They have even reestablished some of their old Sunni tribal groups, one is 'Awakenings Councils', well known for fighting al-Qaeda linked militants. This is a continuation of what Iraq has been going through for hundreds of years," adding, "Sunnis hate Shi'ites, Shi'ites hate Sunnis. Both hate the Americans occupying their country. Al-Qaeda hates both the Sunnis and Shi'ites, and doubly hates the Americans. We should just get our butts the hell out of this country. We never should have come here in the first place. We have been spinning our wheels for six years, and have not accomplished a damn thing. It is an unsolvable place, and has been so since the beginning of time."

Sergeant Bis, smiling, again nodded in agreement, pointing out, "Muqtada al-Sadr has told anyone who wants to hear, 'The United States would remain my enemy until the last drop of my blood.'"

"I remember last August," the corporal contended, "That was when Sadr declared his unilateral truce, saying he wanted to give the Maliki government a chance. His followers then were still part of the Iraqi government. This kept things quiet, up to now, at least for a few months," adding, "The US generals over here took credit, but it was Sadr's orders which really stopped the Sunni-Shi'ite violence."

The Stryker caravan suddenly slowed down. Bis and his men heard a loud explosion. The Sergeant, after looking out his peek hole, discussed it with his driver, found it was not aimed at them, and speed was resumed.

"Sadr and Maliki have this verbal battle going on as to who is going to run the Shi'ite Muslims in the Basra south. Bis said, continuing his conversation with the corporal, "For several years, Sadr militiamen, and other Moslem vigilantes have intimidated, and even killed Basra residents who broke Sadr's strict Moslem rules," adding, "If the US generals, and Maliki, continue their threats to crackdown on the Sadr forces in Basra, there is going to be a big escalation of violence, and it will probably involve us."

"Sadr has a lot of support among all Iraqi Shi'ites," the corporal admitted. "It would be a big mistake for the US Army to try to disband the Sadr's in Basra," adding, "I remember the fighting there back in 2004. Sadr is not an opponent to under rate."

"Muqtada al-Sadr has already warned the generals, if they persist in their crackdown, he would declare, 'Open war until liberation,'" Bis intoned, adding, "I think what the Iraqi government really wants is control of the Basra oil fields."

"I heard that al-Maliki is going to find some way to attack Sadr," another squad man said, entering the conversation, "They are both Shi'ites, and Maliki wants total political control," adding, "It makes no never mind to me," using a Kentucky phrase, "I'm getting out of the army in just a few months."

Another rifleman retorted, "I want to leave both Iraq and the army, but I still have several months to go. I can still hear Sadr saying a few days ago, 'If you don't withdraw from our land,' talking to Americans, 'or set a timetable for withdrawal acceptable to the Iraqi people, we will resist in the way we see fit,' and he added, 'You will always be an enemy.' I believe him."

The Stryker line of eight, again slowed, an action easily discernable by the squad of riflemen, under Bis's tender care.

After talking it over with the driver, Bis told them, "At ease you guys. We are getting close to our forward operating base." Then, giving an order to Corporal Ballard, he said, "Pick out two of our guys for guard duty as soon as we get there."

The Sergeant, with a good view of the road straight ahead, then told his men he could see the outskirts of Baghdad, and we should be in a safe spot soon.

One of the men asked Bis if the caravan could stop, relaying to the rest, "It would sure be refreshing to ride on top the rest of the way."

The Sergeant, thinking it was a good suggestion, radioed ahead, to the officer in charge with the idea, and on a lonely stretch of Iraqi road, the eight vehicle lineup slowed, stopped, looked, and deciding it was safe, released the men from the stifling inside heat.

They, with all the noise of a crowd at a football stadium, got out of the inside of their Strykers, and climbed quickly on top, finding a plentitude of easy seats.

It now was late in the Iraq day, and while the sun was still bright, it was angling to the west, and Iraq was cooling for the night.

The caravan, to accommodate the men, slowed to a reasonable twenty-five miles per hour. The troops gratefully absorbed the welcome cool air, circling in and around their heavy uniforms, even though they were still ordered to keep on their helmets and vests, and to keep their rifles at the ready.

A half-hour later, the Stryker caravan approached their temporary base. The fadings of the semi-twilight darkness of the Iraq coming nighttime appeared to cause the western edges of Baghdad, to the unlearned, as only a beautiful array of colors, rather than the deadly killing place it really was.

The temporary compound, enclosed by heavy strands of barbed wire and sporting a heavy gate, with cement riser backup, brought on a big cheer from the top riding troopers.

The base was heavily guarded by the US all along its perimeter, and the cement block guardhouse was stocked with a multitude of US Army riflemen, all of whom made their voices be known, as the Strykers passed through the gate, and on to their tent home away from home.

As Bis 's vehicle pulled up to the tents, he breathed a sigh of relief, and ordering his squad to attention as they got off their Stryker, told them, "Good job. Take a good rest. Dismissed."

Chapter II –
Sadr City

It was after Bis' Stryker Squad had finished their additional two committed days of extra-hazardous duty, working out of the US Army's temporary deployment base.

Then, after being granted seven days of rest and relaxation, at their safe, permanent barracks in Baghdad's Green Zone, the Squad was issued new orders.

The Squad found itself, at exactly 5:42 a.m., dawn Iraqi time, on April 24, 2008, poised for battle. Bis' Stryker Squad, being one of eight Strykers in their sector, after US directed air strikes, and drone strikes, all set to be unleashed against the enemy. Units of Muqtada al-Sadr's Mahdi Army Militia had been targeted in Baghdad's Shi'ite slum known as Sadr City. The Strykers, following their orders, lurched forward, leading the US Army's attack into the city.

Bis' Strykers usually were given the lead assignment. They were the best.

In this action, the entire 711th Stryker Brigade was totally deployed in this battle. As the battle ensued, there obviously were several unavoidable casualties, mostly between the Sadr militia forces, and the Iraqi forces, also committed to this fight, by the al-Maliki Iraqi government.

The Brigade had been ordered, by US generals, to seal Sadr City off from the rest of Baghdad. The idea was, hopefully, to neutralize Sadr's power base. However, two point five million Shi'ites call the city their home. Many of these residents have become the soldiers fighting in Sadr's Mahdi Army.

"Such neutralization fantasy tales are not realistic," Sergeant Bis thought, as his Stryker moved forward toward the directing explosions of US missiles, predator drones, and US helicopter gunships. The firepower was directed at the Sadr militiamen scrambling to find refuge in this sprawling slum, sited in northeast Baghdad.

Bis could hear the officer who commanded his group, via loudspeakers, warning the residents in the area to keep off the streets, that roadside bombs, set every block or so, would have to be cleared by US Security Forces. The officer also radioed Bis' Stryker, warning him of such bombs, saying, "Seven of the roadside terrorist weapons had already been detonated by the Mahdi," and "Unfortunately, the whole American crew of an American Humvee, escorting a tank, was killed," the officer announced.

"Too late to worry about that," the Sergeant said, almost to himself, and then ordered his driver to increase the speed of Bis' Stryker. Speed was often the key ingredient to avoid blowing up.

The certain sounds of heavy gunfire erupting from the slum neighborhoods met his ears, and Bis could clearly see a few Mahdi fighters lugging rocket propelled grenades, and .50 caliber machine guns into nearby houses and other dens of death.

"Probably stolen from US Army weapons depots," thought Bis of the machine guns, then laughing, *"I'm wrong, they were probably actually issued to these guys before they defected from Maliki's Iraqi Army."*

Bis' Stryker drove into a Sadr City intersection. This one was guarded by an MI-2 army tank, busy lobbing rounds from its heavy cannon, at several cornered Sadr fighters. He also, at this same time, saw a Hellfire missile from a drone explode, taking with it a nearby roadside bomb. It had been placed along the same route as Bis' Stryker had been proceeding. Had it not prematurely exploded, it could have been a fatal encounter.

"God is with us," Bis said aloud to his squad. "Keep your heads down," as their Stryker moved forward to their agreed place of deployment, along with the rest of their battalion. It was directly in the center of Sadr City.

Bis looked back, and could see at least two of the other attacking Strykers, moving at an equal pace behind him.

"The news reporters were right," he declared to his troops, "The Shi'ite residents of Sadr City must have known about this action before we did. A few of them are still lined up stocking up on food and essentials. It is reported that they expect the oncoming fight to be the worst in their memory."

"I hope they are wrong about Mahdi's positioning roadside bombs along Sadr City streets," Corporal Ballard declared.

"Don't bet on that," replied another squad rifleman, "after Prime Minister Maliki ordered Sadr to disband his Mahdi army, or face the consequences, political or military, Sadr's answer was that he will declare 'an open war until liberation.' It should result in one hell-of-a fight – at least for us."

"It looks like we fight," retorted another squadman, "and they hold the coats."

"We are about one mile from where we debark," Sergeant Bis announced. "Remember the biggest thing we are looking for is rogue police, al-Qaeda, or Sadr's militia dressed up in Maliki government police uniforms."

"The Iraq Interior Ministry, which has been given billions of US taxpayer dollars, to train and equip a half million security forces," the corporal contended, "is so corrupt, and so controlled by political patronage, that it is going to be impossible to know who is a Sadr and who is a Maliki."

"Never-the-less," Bis concluded, "we must try, and we must try, starting a few minutes from now. Remember guys, that is an order," adding, "Try to locate some friendly residents."

The Stryker line moved the concluding next mile quickly. Sadr City center appeared eerily deserted, and seemed quiet.

Bis looked out of his Stryker. He ordered his driver to slow and stop. He then told his Squad, "The streets look like they have been cleared of all traffic. Every shop, office, and school I see looks like they are closed."

The Strykers following Bis were pulling into a circle-like attack mode, like the old Western wagon trains used to do. The tactic was one the Brigade had trained diligently for over many months.

"Don't deploy from this Stryker," Bis warned, "until you hear the order directly from me."

Waiting for the rest of the Battalion to arrive, and deploy, Bis began thinking, "*The situation in Iraq was deteriorating. Only four days ago, I was going to shop in the Battalion PX store facility in the American fortified Green Zone Command Center. The area was supposed to be impregnable. All at once, the building, next to where I was paying for a new set of GI underwear, disappeared in a tremendous explosion. When the smoke settled, and the building debris was cleared away, four American former residents of the Green Zone were dead. They were the victims of the high explosive rockets, fired with ease, into the Green Zone from the adjacent Sadr City, by the Mahdi Army.*"

Bis laughed, as he remembered hurried up orders being given to American Embassy staffers, "*Stay under hardened cover. Sleep in cots in the reinforced embassy structures, and, you are required to wear body armor and a helmet anytime you venture outside the structures in the Green Zone."* Bis chuckled, remembering how the gal from Cincinnati looked so cute in a Stryker helmet and a mini skirt.

One of the Strykers in his deployment group suddenly let loose with its heavy cannons and machine guns. They were aimed at an abandoned shop which looked empty, but suddenly bristled with Sadr militiamen bearing AK-47's and rocket propelled grenades.

Bis ordered his two squadmen trained in firing his Stryker's heavy cannons into action, and to focus their weapons on the deadly shop.

The Squad clearly, could hear returning rocket propelled grenades bounce off the metal carriage of their vehicle, as the squadmen opened up, and blasted the scrambling militia. At the same time, Bis could hear US drones, and US helicopter gunships joining in the assault.

"There goes the last of a dirty dozen," Bis exclaimed, as the abandoned shop became dust, and the twelve or so Sadrites also became dust.

Bis, looking again out his windows at the Battalion deployment, and finding it still in the forming process, told his Squad, "Stay down. We are not ready to go yet."

As Bis viewed the shop debris in front of the Stryker, he could see the bodies of a few of the dead Mahdis and commented, "It looks like two of them are wearing US uniforms. They must have tried to disguise themselves, probably as interpreters."

"Lots of GI's lost their lives, being fooled by such disguises," Corporal Ballard observed, "GI's are much too trusting."

The radio crackled, and kicked out some information that only a few blocks down from their vehicles a woman suicide, pushing a cart in front of the local police station, killed five Iraqi policemen. The radio followed that up, reporting that a parked car had exploded as a Stryker, from a different outfit, was passing, and it was disabled, but all the riflemen were okay.

The radio's hum, lulled Bis into remembering, *"The reason for today's Brigade size attack on Sadr City, was to isolate it, and to clear it of Sadrites, to free up the Green Zone of those lethal rocket attacks. But, like the Corporal says, 'Sunnis hate Shi'ites. Shi'ites hate Sunnis. The Saudi al-Qaeda hates both. But all of them are agreed on one thing. All of them hate the American occupiers.' Day by day, conditions in Iraq continue to get worse. The longer we stay here, the more neighbor hates neighbor."*

Bis paused, *"The US Army's reason to stay here is because Bush II, the neo-cons, and the Israeli general staff, wants America to fight their war against Iran,"* adding, *"All of it is senseless, and it is bankrupting America. We must leave, and soon."*

As if reading Bis' mind, the Corporal commented aloud, "Three thousand eight hundred sixty-one GI's dead. Twenty-eight thousand seven hundred ninety GI's wounded. One hundred fifty thousand Iraqi civilians killed. Four million Iraqi's fleeing Iraq. As

Bush says, 'Because we acted, the world is better,'" adding, "How much better can it get?"

Bis broke into an almost hysterical laugh. He stopped long enough to ask the Corporal, "Do you know what a Tomahawk Cruise missile costs?"

The Corporal made no reply.

Bis immediately answered his own question, saying, "They cost one point five million each. That is what it costs the American taxpayers on March 3, 2008, when two of them were fired at a supposed target in the town of Dodley in Somalia, in an effort to quiet the elites clambering for America to do something."

"What happened?" asked a squad rifleman, listening to the conversation.

"The two Tomahawk missiles, in a valiant defense of Somalia killed a dastardly Moslem, probably a Sadrist Islamic donkey," Bis replied.

The Strykers rolled in unscripted laughter, which continued unabated, until all at once, the radio rattled out an order, "This is the Brigade Commander," it relayed. "We are ready to proceed. Squad leaders, deploy your men. Keep them in a single line, and combine all squads in an attack formation at the entrance to the former school building. It is depicted on your map as Point A. Begin now."

"Okay, Squad, move out," Bis ordered, going to the front of his troops as they began deploying down the back Stryker ramp. "Follow me."

Corporal Ballard took up his normal position in the back of the Stryker Squad, as they moved out onto the vacated, Sadr City street.

The odd three story school building loomed ahead, like a prehistoric monster.

Bis told his Squad, "Keep an eye open for surprises."

The Sergeant led his troops, moving them from one assortment of battle debris to another, pausing at each pile to determine the safest time to again move forward.

At the school entrance, the Squad again moved forward, with Bis yelling, "Follow me to the open side of the far wall," referring to a brick wall, surrounding the school building, which had been shattered in several spots by previous cannon balls.

A strange silence, maybe only a quirk of Bis' imagination, seemed then to overcome him. It was an eerie kind of quiet that shut out all of the other ear splitting surrounding battle noise. It only lasted a brief second.

That bit of quiet allowed Bis alone to hear what sounded like the report of a single rifle shot. He heard it as it whistled past him.

Bis, on a hunch, looked up to the windows on the third floor of the school building. He saw, what looked like to him, the muzzle of a rifle. He also, ominously, glanced back over his Squad. As if by an omen, Corporal John Ballard, unexpectedly, suddenly stood straight up. He grabbed frantically at his neck, allowing his rifle to fall, as he tried to stop an interfering foreign object that had entered his body. To do so, he fell forward, unconscious.

"The Corporal's been hit," a Squadman hollered.

"Keep moving forward," Bis yelled.

The Squad, following the Sergeant's orders, did move into secure spots behind a portion of the protecting wall, as Bis told them to do. He then ordered, "Concentrate your fire," pointing, "on the second window on the right, third floor. I saw a sniper."

That done, Bis then moved back the few open feet to where Ballard now lay prostrate. He grabbed both of his legs, and in one turning motion, rolled both he and the Corporal behind a few pieces of broken pavement cement, which gave them both some protection.

As Bis tried to remove Ballard's bulletproof vest, he could see the sniper's shot had found its mark.

It was a little above the vest, and it angled downward. The Corporal opened his eyes, but said nothing.

Neither the unmistakable noise made by the rapid firing of seven of his Squad's automatic rifles, all concentrated at the school window Bis had ordered blasted, aroused Ballard, nor did the rousting shouts from his buddies, "We got him, the dirty bastard."

The Sergeant was able to remove the vest. He could see the wound had hit a vital spot. It was fatal.

The Corporal, exerting a great effort, was once more able to open his eyes. With an even greater effort, he formed a sort of quirky smile, and looking directly at his Sergeant friend, managed to say, "It was only a few months to go." As he breathed his last breath, the Corporal's eyes closed, but the quirky smile remained.

"Why? Why? Why?" the Sergeant yelled to the sky.

It was loud enough to attract the notice of the entire Stryker Battalion.

The Sergeant was far enough away, however, that the tears blinding his eyes could not be seen.

Chapter III –
Ode To
Corporal Ballard

A full week had elapsed. *"Seven days,"* Sergeant Ian von Bismarck thought to himself, sitting alone in a vacated, empty barracks on the edge of his GI cot, in the Green Zone. *"I must get this letter out to Ballard's mother. I owe it to him."*

He continued thinking, *"What can you say to a mother who has lost her own son. John so wanted to survive; to complete this Iraqi tour; to complete his enlistment; to get back to his home in Oregon; to marry the girl he was confirmed with in 'Our Lady's Catholic Church'; to start a family. These were the goals he told me about."*

Bis paused and began writing these words, "John Ballard, by his undaunted courage, fighting spirit, and unwavering devotion to duty - - - in the face of - - - ," Bis stopped, put down his pen. He re-read the words which the army suggested might be appropriate for this kind of letter, - - - "gallantly gave his life for his country - - - great credit upon himself - - - upholding the highest traditions of the United States."

After pondering these select words for a brief period, Bis told himself, out loud, almost in a yell, *"Bullshit,"* adding, *"Ballard and my squad were in Sadr City because Maliki, the Iraqi Prime Minister was under pressure from General David Petraeus, to militarily confront the Sadr Mahdi Army, and the Shi'ite resistance fighters. It was to push the Sadrists beyond the range where they could fire rockets into the Green Zone. But the main motive was to seal off the area, to neutralize Muqtada al-Sadr's control of the thirty seats he held in the Iraqi Parliament, which kept the Shi'ite majority. It was to cement Maliki's control of his shaky government."*

The Sergeant reluctantly got up, paced back and forth a few feet, then abruptly returned to his cot. He again told himself, *"Maliki and Petraeus' assault stalled because the Mahdi Army put up an unexpected resistance. One thousand of Maliki's newly trained Iraqi soldiers refused to fight the Mahdis. Several local Maliki trained Iraqi police officers, also refused to fight,"* adding, *"These reluctant warriors were either intimidated by Sadr, or were Sadr's loyalists."*

He continued thinking, *"The upshot of it was Maliki had to call in other Iraqi units, and had to call out to the American Army for help. Several American airstrikes, missiles, and the fire power of the Strykers saved Maliki's rear end. It also sent several score Iraqi citizens to the hospital, killed a hundred of Sadr's fighters, along with the death of a couple hundred of Maliki's Army.*

"Corporal Ballard's death, in this Maliki attack against Sadr, at any rate, had nothing to do with – 'devotion to duty' – upholding the highest traditions of America – and most of all – 'sacrificing his life for his country,'" Bis told himself. *"It has to do, alone, with Bush II's continuing morality play, which is to 'stay the course' in Iraq. Bush II, with the advice of his handlers, has now cast, as the star, and main character of this bit of acting, General David Petraeus, the commander of all US Forces in Iraq. This so-called idol is billed as the savior of all by Bush agreeing American politicians, and of all the Israeli politicians. Those who want the war to continue. The American controlled media have so glamorized Petraeus, that now, if anyone tries to criticize him, it is characterized as a kind of blasphemy. He represents the fading false hope, that says – don't lose heart – we can still win.*

"Win what?" Bis continued to ponder, adding, *"I think the bigger reason Petraeus is in Iraq is he will back Bush II and the Israeli's in insisting on attacking Iran,"* adding, *"Bush II people keep blaming Iran for arming Sadr's militia, and killing American soldiers, but in the battles I have been in, I have seen as many American weapons as those attributed to Iran. Both are easily gettable on the Black Market. It would be better if General Petraeus should have to answer how weapons which were issued to Maliki's Army, wound up in Sadr's Army."*

The Sergeant continued thinking, *"Also, why haven't the Democrat Senators cut off the money to*

Iraq? *They have the power. Are they also in the pocket of the Israelis?" adding, "Maybe they hope, like Pontius Pilate, they can wash their hands and be done with it."*

Bis could not repress a spontaneous laugh, as he thought about the whole situation, remembering back in March of 2007, when Bush first brought Petraeus to Iraq. Bis reminded himself, talking to the empty barracks, *"Petraeus, in his usual phony, ingratiating way, reported to Admiral William Fallon, his boss in Iraq. Fallon, a veteran of years in the Navy, was not only an old salt, but had flown many hazardous missions, and experienced many hectic aircraft return landings on various Navy flight decks, in his forty-one years of distinguished service to his nation. He rose to the heights in command, including one of America's most important, the Pacific Command. Admiral Fallon was well known to the troops as intellectually and operationally aggressive. He did not pull his punches. If anyone became his military enemy, it was because they did not do their assigned military job," adding, "After Petraeus had reported in, Fallon confided, confidentially to an associate, depicting the General as an, 'Ass kissing little chicken shit.' This apt distain of Petraeus soon became common knowledge to all the agreeing GI's in Iraq."*

The Sergeant again picked up his pen, and began writing, *"Dear Mrs. Ballard: I had the good fortune to have John Ballard, as not only a respected member of my squad, but as the man who was second in command, and who, all of us without question, could rely on in any situation. He was our never bending oak tree, in the torrid, barren, Iraqi forest. I am personally aware of* at least three occasions where John, by his unwavering devotion to protecting his squad, and because of his undaunted courage, was able to save the lives of three of his fellow riflemen, by striking the enemy first, and destroying them as the Iraqis were readying themselves to ambush John's riflemen buddies."

Bis dropped his pen again, asking himself, *"Is this what I want to say? It is the truth, but will his mother be comforted by it?"*

The Sergeant, unsure, thumbed through some of the personal items John Ballard had kept in his footlocker. Overlooked before was a simple prayer card. It was labeled, "A Prayer to Saint Michael". On the back of the card was printed, "Catholics are invited to pray to Saint Michael in defense against the forces of darkness." The prayer also entreated the "Archangel to be our protection against wickedness."

"John was a highly devoted, practicing Catholic," Bis reasoned. *"It must be assumed his mother is too. John must have believed in, and, on occasion, recited the prayer. He certainly realized that in Iraq he was in the middle of all the forces of darkness in the world, leeringly gathered together by Lucifer to continue his constant production of murders, killings, assassinations, and the unbridled release of brutality. It was not only against the Iraqi people, but, over and over again, it took a disproportionate share of American service people."*

Bis, inspired, revisited the letter to Ballard's mother, telling her of the strong close feelings all of the squad had for John, and ending the missive, writing, *"You can be assured that your son was the*

25

personification of the Prayer to Saint Michael. John uttered it often, in so many words, entreating all of us to do all we could to destroy the persistent forces of darkness and wickedness, which we all discovered in Iraq. It was for these reasons that John gave his life. It was for the squad."

Bis folded the letter, put it in its envelope, interposing to himself, *"That is the truth. It is how Ballard really felt in his heart."*

As the Sergeant complete the letter, his squad members began returning to re-habitate the empty barracks. He had, just a few hours ago, sent them all out, along with their M4 Colt carbines, each rifle with a capability of firing seven hundred to nine hundred fifty bullets per minute. This piece of metal and plastic was the staff of life for all of them. The carbines were to be newly fitted with a thermo imaging devise. Bis hoped it would be of help to protect them.

Roger Tooley, a squad member showing a dour face, came up to Bis, bringing him some bad news, saying, "I talked to a Brigade sergeant. He told me that Maliki's Iraqi Army is not doing the job in Sadr City, and that probably our squad will be ordered back in."

"I don't wonder," Bis replied. "Prime Minister Nouri al-Maliki was on the tube yesterday, telling Muqtada al-Sadr that his military action against Sadr's followers in Sadr City would end only when they, not only surrendered, but also had given up his weapons," adding, "Bush II, and his Secretary of State's actions to publicly praise Maliki for confronting Sadr's Army did not help."

Bis continued, "The Mahdi Army is estimated to consist of sixty thousand fighters, and of those five thousand are veteran, highly trained troops. Such numbers can put up a convincing, long, drawn out fight."

"Well it is obvious, the Baath-ist Sunni's, who used to run Iraq under Saddam Hussein, are elated with the Sadr attacks," Tooley retorted, adding, "What Maliki, Petraeus, and Bush II, evidently don't take into account, is that Sadr also has significant political support in the oil fields, oil lines, and ports in the Shi'ite south."

"Along with his controlling US taxpayer financed Iraqi social services, and medical clinics," the Sergeant pointed out."

"The Brigade sergeant also told me that both sides were using innocent Iraqi civilians as human shields in Sadr City, and that Sadr's forces were showing little sign of weakening. In fact, one bunch of Sadrists attacked a US outpost in Sadr City with mortars and machine guns," adding, "While the GI's beat them back, it shows they still have wallop."

"Sadr and Maliki are mainly both trying to gain political control of the Shi'ite areas in Iraq," Bis agreed, adding, "For Maliki to try to exert this level of control and siphon off an area containing half of Baghdad's population, does not show clear thinking. It is a politically motivated attempt to try to influence the Shi'ite vote in the scheduled fall elections in Iraq."

Tooley nodded in agreement, saying, "Petraeus and Bush II brag about the effect of their so-called surge, and how adding thirty thousand GI's to Iraq in

December of 2007, has turned the war around, but the ever constant killings seem the same to me," adding, "but as I read the situation, what has really happened, is a sort of ethnic cleansing."

"What do you mean?" asked Bis.

"Back in 2003, when we invaded Iraq, forty-five percent of Baghdad's neighborhoods were mostly Sunni, with the remainder being mixed. Now, sixty-five percent of Baghdad's neighborhoods are, almost exclusively Shi'ite, and only about thirty percent remain Sunni. Five percent remain mixed, and survive because American Forces happen to be based in those areas."

He continued, "The Shi'ite death squads have obviously done their duty. They have killed, assassinated, or chased out of the country, at least two million refugees, mostly Sunni. Talk about a neighborly way of doing things. It is a clearly classic ethnic cleansing job."

Bis smiled, agreeing, and at the same time thinking, *"This guy might be a good replacement for Ballard. He knows how to think, and keeps up with the world,"* but, in answer to the ethnic cleansing observation, the Sergeant, after pausing, offered, "It cannot be denied that both the Sunnis and the Shi'ites used the excuse of an American occupation to also murder hundreds of the several centuries' old, Iraqi Christian population. They, without any remorse, drove a million of them right out of the country. They also did it right under the noses of the American generals, and with such a non-challenge, that it could only be thought of as a policy which was approved by Bush, and his handlers, or at least, disregarded," adding, "Talk about your ethnic murders, how about these religious murders," adding, "But, if you think about it, the underlying main reason for the temporary lull in Sunni killing Shi'ite, and Shi'ite killing Sunni, is Petraeus' new willingness to confederate the US Forces with the very Saddam Sunni Forces, Bush II, and his handlers originally invaded Iraq to destroy in 2003."

"That is the absolute truth," Roger Tooley attested. "I remember when I was in Iran in 2006, several Sunni chiefs in Iraq, at that time, told a few of the US Intelligence officers that were my bosses at the time, that the chiefs would, for a price, no longer support al-Qaeda terrorist actions in Iraq. They were miffed because the al-Qaeda had been terrorizing some of their Sunnis, but, it was mostly because al-Qaeda snubbed and by-passed the Sunni chiefs."

Bis looked up with surprise, appreciating that one of his squad members would be able to process that kind of information. Before giving Tooley a comment on his al-Qaeda revelation, the Sergeant asked him, "I need a Corporal. Would you take the job if I recommended you? It would mean a promotion and more money."

Tooley responded, saying, "As you probably know, I have been a corporal before, and a sergeant before," adding, "I ran into trouble with dumb sergeants, and dumb officers," laughing, "Its my Irish temper. But I like you, Sergeant Bismarck. If you can stand me, I will work hard for you."

Bis smiling, replied, "You are hired. Welcome. I will put in the necessary paperwork this afternoon," as he, at the same time, shook Tooley's hand.

"Now, as you pointed out, the surge was mostly the Sunni chief's agreeing to re-combat the al-Qaeda, I agree, but it was not so much a voluntary action, as it was an out and out bribe."

Sergeant Bis continued, "By February of 2008, Petraeus had already enlisted sixty-five thousand 'Awakening Councils', Sunnis, mainly because the US taxpayers were furnishing them salaries of three hundred dollars per month, a fortune in Iraq. The Sunni chiefs also were given bribes, in the form of two hundred fifty million dollars in reconstruction grants."

"I've got twelve years in this man's army," conceded Tooley, "and I have never seen such corruption as you have right here in Iraq. The disease doesn't take sides. It affects everybody. It's a way of life," adding, "Anybody with any brains can see that there will never be an Iraqi nation. There will only be a section controlled by the Sunnis, allied, and supported by Saudi Arabia, and a section controlled by the Shi'ites, allied and supported by Iran, and in between – continued suicide assassinations, killings, and bombings."

"I agree," Bis interposed. "The Sunni bribe will only last so long, and then the whole country will return to turmoil and self destruction," adding, "The most that can be said of the Bush II-Petraeus bribe is, it would allow American forces to, unilaterally declare victory, and quickly remove itself from Iraq."

Tooley laughed involuntarily, replying, "You don't think Israel and Bush II's handlers would allow that, do you?"

"There is always a chance," Bis conceded.

"Like Voltaire wrote, 'chance is a word void of sense, nothing can exist without a cause.'"

"Do you know who Voltaire was?" the Sergeant responded.

"He was an intelligent Frenchman, back when there were intelligent Frenchmen," Tooley offered smiling.

CHAPTER IV - OTTO

The Brigade Sergeant was right. Roger Tooley was right. Bis' Stryker Unit was ordered to go back into the al-Maliki-Petraeus versus al-Sadr Shi'ite showdown, in Sadr City.

Sergeant Ian von Bismarck was ordered to report to a battalion huddle of Strykers, where the outline of the coming plan of battle was presented by Bis' platoon and company officers.

At the meeting, Bis was also given permission to use Tooley as an "acting" corporal, pending final approval of his paperwork.

Back at his barracks, Bis called Tooley to a squad meeting and told him, of both decisions, inquiring at the same time, "Where are you from?" as Tooley had a definite Southern accent.

"I'm from Macon, Georgia," Tooley admitted, "and while I don't have an Irish brogue, I do have an Irish temper," adding, "But I will accept the corporal's job, and I guarantee that I will be a good Southern boy, because I both like you, and I respect you. If that should change, I'll let you know."

"That's fair enough," Bis replied. "Remember, it is my standing policy to protect the Squad first. All other things are 'other'. Understand that?"

"Agreed," Tooley retorted, adding, "What ruckus is going on in Sadr City? Why send us?"

"Even after a several week offensive, both in Sadr City, and in the Shi'ite south, by Maliki's Army," Bis replied, "the Iraqi premier is not able to eliminate, neutralize, or sideline Sadr, and his Mahdi Army.

"In fact, the Mahdis beat the hell out of Maliki, and he now has to be rescued by calling in the American Army."

Bis continued, "Even with the US firepower, Sadr still is lobbing hundreds of rockets and mortars, as we all well know, into our Green Zone sanctuary."

"While most don't bother us," confided the corporal, "two civilian contractors were killed yesterday, and my buddies at Brigade level, admitted that things are so bad, the US, not only has to throw air power and special units into the action, but it is getting to a crucial, decisive point. This is probably why the Strykers were ordered in."

"We are ordered to deploy, but not until tomorrow morning, at 'O'-six hundred," Bis disclosed. "We move after Sadr City has been saturated and clobbered by helicopter gunships, Air Force missiles, and drone missiles."

Bis, pausing, ordered, "Corporal, give the Squad the word. Get them ready."

After instructing Tooley, Bis, exhausted after the non-stop marathon, retreated to his semi-private area. This was a privilege only given to the Stryker Squad's First Sergeants and only in the Green Zone barracks.

Bis stretched out on his Spartan army cot, intending a quick nap. As he tried to push sleep, he became more awake. His mind became fixed on a comment by one of the brigade staff officers, who had taken him aside at the just finished briefing. He wanted to know, which brought a Bis chuckle, if he was descended from German royalty.

He was born Ian Otto von Bismarck. The full name was necessarily shown on his official military papers, but he had never used his given middle name, Otto, or the title, von, in his usual dealings. *"In fact,"* he thought, *"he doubted whether any Squad member knew his full name."*

Bis turned on his side, in the reluctant cot, thinking, *"Actually, he really was a distant, distant relative of the historic German-Prussian soldier, Otto von Bismarck, the Kaiser's top military and political consultant in the Prussian dominated 1870's – 1890's. He remembered his father telling him of his purported Prussian ancestry, and relating, his Great-Great-Grandfather was a Prussian officer, and also a third cousin to the great Otto. His Great-Grandfather was the third born son to the officer, and, as such, would have no royal advantage staying in the German hierarchy, even with the name von Bismarck. Thus, this third born son immigrated to America at the age of twenty. He landed in New York in June of 1873. At first, he tried to succeed in various businesses, but did* not. *He married a New York school teacher in 1887, at the ripe old age of thirty-five. His Grandfather was born of the marriage in 1889, their only child, and both of his Grandfather's parents died in the 1917 flu epidemic. His Prussian officer uncles, in Germany, were both killed, unmarried, on the Western front during the First World War, as was their father. His Grandfather, thus, alone, and with no family in New York, heard of the enticing black dirt of Iowa, and decided to be a farmer. He, thus, in 1920, invested what little life savings he had, as a down payment on one hundred sixty acres of land in Newtown, Iowa, as a thirty-one-year-old, non-experienced, first time agriculturalist."*

Bis rolled over again, ending on his back, contemplating the ceiling, but remembering his father's continuing saga of his Bismarck origins. His father further related, *"During the 1920's, when farm prices were good, and with advice from his generous neighbors, his Grandfather made a reasonable living, and even was able to marry an Iowa 'old maid' in 1927. The resulting birth of his father in 1931,"* he admitted, *"was a pleasant surprise. However, it was followed by the great American depression of 1932. As a result, his Grandfather lost the farm to the bank. To eke out a living, his in-laws ponied up some seed money to buy a small grocery store in Newtown. His Grandparents ran that until 1955, when, unfortunately, his Grandmother and Grandfather, extending their string of bad luck, pulled their delivery car out into the town's main highway connection, in front of a semi-trailer truck, making my father, at age twenty-four, an orphan with a grocery store. He was, at the time, a student at a local college, called Northern Iowa, majoring in English Literature."* His father related, *"He reluctantly was summoned home to run the small grocery store, as it was his source of income."* Bis then recalled, *"He remained at the store, however, and managed to marry the town librarian in 1970, staying single until age thirty-nine. The library, his first love, is where he spent most of his time."*

Bis sighed, and again involuntarily turned over in his sleepless cot, thinking, *"The neighbors told me they were surprised that I was ever born of the marriage, on March 10, 1972, as both my mother and my father's main interest in life was literary. They neglected running the store. Discussing and reading instead, Shakespeare, the classics, and sopping up any available English literature topics, along with his mother's love for American writers. They so loved this voluntary departure from the norm, unusual in a small city like Newtown, that customers usually had to remind them to restock some of their shelves, in their untended grocery store.*

"Fortunately for me," laughed Bis to himself, *"they did find time for procreation."*

Pleasantly remembering his childhood, Bis could recall spending most of his growing up days sitting at a small desk in the store, or at the library, with his mother, either reading classics, or being read English literature by both his father and mother.

"His mother's affinity for American writers prompted her to emphasize American history to Bis. He became unusually aware of the revolutionary

founders, the Civil War leaders, the stumbling into the First World War, and all the American history, and American villains, and heroes in between."

Bis, uncomfortable again, tried to stretch out his legs on the unforgiving cot, remembering that his father's greater interest was in reading Shakespeare, the classics, and exploring European history, which happened to include a search into the Otto von Bismarck genealogy.

The Sergeant, still sleepless, concluded, *"His father was so very proud of the 'Otto' connection, and his search was obviously self satisfying, as was proven when he named Bis, Ian Otto von Bismarck. It was a compromise,"* he explained to anyone who would listen, *"While his wife preferred 'Ian', she then relented to using the middle name, 'Otto'. His father said it restored, somewhat, a Prussian royalty connection of their Prussian officer ancestor's third degree cousinship to the world renowned, Otto von Bismarck. The First World War, he reasoned, had destroyed all the officer's heirs, except his remaining American son.*

"Whatever the reason," Bis thought, *"He had no quarrel with the name, except when he had to use it fully, as he had done a few times. It had always brought on the inevitable questions of Prussian royalty, which then were followed up with unfounded accusations or suggestions of Prussian loyalty."*

"This would not do," the Sergeant thought, *"He was now a one hundred percent all American boy, and any Prussian ancestry was interesting, but only incidental.*

"Beyond that," he thought, *"Since his father died when Bis was only age eleven, he had been much more influenced in his thinking by his mother."*

He remembered, at the time, how difficult it was to exchange his literary life for that of a grocery store operator, as that is what he had to do. *"His mother,"* he recalled, *"could only spend part of her time at the store, in order to keep her desired position at the library.*

"Fortunately," Bis continued to remember, *"in the friendly atmosphere of Newtown, the customers usually waited on themselves anyway, and many times they left cash with a note on the counter, which remained,"* he laughed, *"unmolested, in payment."*

Bis chuckled, thinking, *"I doubt whether this kind of business neglect would survive in today's self satisfying world. That was no longer a problem, as growing to adulthood, his helping to tend the store, was no longer necessary."*

Bis recalled, during that period, *"His mother was able to receive her Social Security, along with some Social Security of her deceased husband. She was also allowed to work part time at the library, which gave her sufficient income to live on, freeing Bis of any obligations."*

"The grocery store had lasted, providing sustenance and income, for Bis and his mother, however, fortunately, until Bis graduated from Newtown's high school, in 1989."

He chuckled, as he remembered, *"He had just a few days prior, received an acceptance letter from a small Lutheran college in St. Paul, Minnesota, awarding him a full scholarship, based on his income, his high school grades, and his high SAT scores, along with a job working in the college kitchen. About the same time, the wholesale grocery corporation that had for years provided the stock for their store went out of business, which spelled doom for their Newtown, non-competitive grocery. The main culprit was the recent arrival of a 'big box', super grocery, and everything else, corporation, operating in Newtown's sister city, twenty-five miles down the road. It did not take long to cause most of the local grocery stores to close down in a fifty mile radius."*

Bis, then thought about his journey through college, which, while relevant to his "Otto" name, never came to be, as Bis, mentally and physically exhausted, succumbed to the deep sleep that suddenly overcame him. This lasted until he reluctantly opened his eyes to Corporal Tooley's gentle shaking of his shoulder, telling the Sergeant, "Wake up, Sergeant, its 3:00 a.m., we have to motor up our Strykers in an hour to be ready for a 6:00 a.m. deployment."

Bis, back to reality, sat up with a suddenness that surprised both him and the Corporal, the latter interposing, "Relax Sergeant, Sadr promised he would wait for us."

Bis smiled, wiping sleep out of his eyes, and then reaching for his boots, commented, "We best not keep him, or the battalion, waiting," adding, "Is the Squad up and getting ready?"

"They are coming," replied Tooley. "A few needed some extra prodding," as he left the Sergeant in order to police his Squad buddies.

"Good choice," Bis thought, contemplating the Corporal, "He will do just fine."

Continuing his thoughts, as he put on the extensive military garb necessary to participate in Iraqi combat, *"Don't worry Mister Prime Minister Nouri al-Maliki, of the sovereign state of Iraq, which is not really sovereign, we will save your tail, and even give Bush and Petraeus some bragging rights,"* adding, *"not to support you gentlemen, but to preserve us."*

Chapter V – Wall Street

Bis happened to glance at the small calendar scotch taped to the side of his footlocker, as he finished donning all the military paraphernalia necessary to participate in the ongoing combat in Iraq.

"May 1, 2008," Bis declared out loud. *"Communist Day. Very appropriate. That's what we have in Iraq, an Emir-Communist way of life. The only difference is whether it's a Sunni-Emir-Communist group, a Sadr-Emir-Shi'ite-Communist group, or a Maliki-Emir-Shi'ite-Communist group. In the end it's all the same, all anti-American, and all totalitarian."*

"Did you say something?" Tooley asked.

"Not important," Bis responded. "Is the squad ready? Did you check over their M-4 carbines?""Yes and yes," Tooley answered, smiling.

Bis then radioed his platoon officer and reported, "Seventh Squadron all ready sir."

The radio replied, rattling out, "Start your Strykers, and move them to the mobilization area, Sergeant."

"Move out," yelled Bis.

It did not take long for all the squadrons of the 711th Stryker Brigade to form up.

Bis' Squad, as usual, was ordered to take the point. The squadron moved out, destined for the southern Tharwa and Jamilla neighborhoods of Sadr City.

"Where are we headed?" yelled a squadsman.

"To the south part of Muqtada's city," Bis replied. "We are going for the southern exposure vacation option, along beautiful downtown al-Quds Street."

"Some vacation," the squadsman answered. "That's where the American Army engineers are putting up the concrete wall."

"You got it," Bis retorted. "Three miles of concrete. Somehow the Iranians who live in Sadr City resent the US Army constructing an ugly, thirty foot, concrete slab wall cutting off their main thoroughfare. I wonder why?"

"This time I agree with the generals," Tooley offered. Sadr's Chinese-made .107 mm Katyusha have a range of about five miles. The Green Zone, our home away from home, is a bit more than five miles from the new wall, so maybe we can get some sleep now and again."

It was still mostly dawnishly dark, as the long string of Strykers, efficiently moved along the now familiar main Baghdad streets, leading to Sadr City.

Bis cautiously looked out his bulletproof windows and peek holes, commenting, as things appeared quiet, "Each one of those concrete slabs weigh in at twelve thousand pounds. Just the uniqueness of the operation draws Shi'ite expected sniper fire," adding, "A three mile wall, however, would effectively cut off infiltration from side streets, and channel traffic through the proposed three major checkpoints, where vehicles can be searched for bombs and weapons."

"I'm all for protecting GI's," Tooley commented, "but if they really want a good solution, why don't we just all go home, and let Sadr and Maliki divide up this barren piece of nothing."

Bis smiled at the thought, and was about to comment that it looked like the Squad was about at the halfway point, when the familiar, unique noise of a US guided missile whistled overhead, followed quickly by another. A minute later, two explosions signaled that the missiles had struck somewhere ahead, causing someone, or something, lethal problems.

"Those must be some of the prelims they promised us," Bis yelled over the increasing noise. We should next be hearing some US Apache helicopters coming on with Hellfire rockets. That also was promised us."

The Stryker slowed and then made a sharp turn west onto al-Quds, the Iraqi street where the action in Sadr City was taking place.

"Gentlemen," Bis said chuckling, "Welcome to Wall Street, an Iraqi first. No stocks, no bonds, but a lot of terminal investment."

Up ahead, several of the Iraqi houses, shops, and what used to be a medical clinic along "Wall Street" were leveled, reduced to rubble by the US guided missiles and rockets.

"Wow," said the Stryker driver, "I hope there were no civilians in that mess."

"A problem you run into when the enemy is shooting at you from the same houses, shops, and medical clinics," Bis declared, adding, "We can expect to get sniper fire targeting our Strykers soon. Don't do anything heroic until you receive my orders."

The Sergeant's combat vehicle, as it approached the concrete wall construction area, was directed to proceed at top operating speed, seeking to gain the protective cover of those sections of wall that were already erected, pulling to the far end to make room for all the incoming Strykers. They did so, and as was predicted, sniper fire could be heard bouncing off their Stryker, steadily increasing to a constant ping.

This continued until a sergeant from the troops that had guarded the wall overnight came on the radio, bragging, "We are the fighting devils of the 1st Battalion, 13th Armor Regiment, the Bradley Armored Vehicle Bad Boys, welcoming you all to an Iraqi breakfast."

His voice was immediately drowned out by volleys of rifle fire, machine guns, and the pom poms of the Bradley's .25 mm guns, further leveling the remaining half destroyed houses into more rubble on that unfortunate, north side of al-Quds Street.

The radio then blared, "How do you Stryker guys like those apples?"

"I'm a believer," Bis told the Bradley Boys by radio. "Thanks for the help. Our number one Stryker is directly behind your Bradley vehicle. When you are ready to take off, let us know. We will cover you with our M-240 .50 caliber machine guns. My troops will also move in to take over your exact positions with as much fire power as our M-4's can muster."

"Thanks," the Bradley sergeant replied. "Right now, we are waiting for the engineering crew slated to put up concrete slabs on this good day. My boys are dug in around the main crane, so that is where you will be," adding, "Should be a hot day for you, the crane always draws lots of attention. I heard the Sadr guys blew up a joint security station last night, a few miles south of here, in the Tharwa District. They drove a captured US Army truck up behind the station, complete with, already installed launcher rails on it. They lobbed several rockets over the station's protective wall, destroying the place. A lot of US troops there, but no fatal injuries. The truck got away."

"Sadr's boys get very innovative at times," Bis retorted over his radio, "They know we are unlikely to fire on an American truck."

"Keep an eye on the rooftops of the second set of buildings," the Brigade sergeant warned. "That is where the new sniper fire is likely to come from," adding, "I don't know what's keeping the engineers? I hope they got past the roadside bombs."

In an irritated voice, the Bradley sergeant declared, "I'm going to sign off for a few minutes. I want to call up to my command about this delay, and get the word on Muqtada al-Sadr's latest moves. If the engineers are stopped, I want to know. My boys did their duty. They want to get some sleep."

As the sergeant signed off, Bis ordered all of his anxious squad, "Relax. We are going to be Stryker bound for some time yet," adding, "Keep your rifles handy. Remember, they do the unexpected."

Corporal Tooley, noting the delay, made his way forward, asking, "Did I hear the Bradley guy talking about 'The' Mister Sadr, the invisible Emir?"

"He seems to be everywhere, and yet nowhere," Bis complained.

"Don't cut him short," responded the Corporal, "When I worked with intelligence, it was clear that Sadr is a home grown leader, with genuine support from Shi'ites all over Iraq. He is the son of a revered Ayatollah, martyred by Hussein's Ba'ath regime, and also he was one of a few who refused to leave Iraq during Saddam's reign."

"Not only that," Tooley continued, "Sadr's group is given credit for setting up a popular Shi'ite social service network in many Iraqi cities. The natives love him, and with good reason."

"I thought Sadr is supposed to be in Iran," Bis contended. "What about that?" adding, "The Secretary of State labeled him a coward, hiding in Iran."

"That was dumb," Tooley declared. "It will only strengthen his support. Sadr is actively attending the Shi'ite's top Islamic theology school at Qom, in Iran, and has been for about a year. The Iraqis understand this. They also understand, when he finishes those studies, actually an indoctrination," Tooley admitted, "he could well be raised to Iraq's Chief Ayatollah."

"I thought Ayatollah al-Sistani was the Iraqi Emir boss," Bis replied. "The generals have reported that Sistani has asked Sadr to disband his army," adding, "I also thought Qom is where Iran's Ayatollah Khomeini has his Iranian capitol, heading the group that actually controls Iran."

"Brigade intelligence also tells me, through a sergeant I know, and they have actually put Sistani traveling to Qom to talk specifically to Sadr, and advising him not to disband his Mahdi Army," Tooley replied. "Also it is imperative for any contending Ayatollah to spend at least ten years at the prestigious Islamic school. Khomeini did."

"You don't mean to tell me," laughed Bis, "that an Ayatollah will tell a lie."

"All the time," Tooley responded. "Plus much more," adding, "Sadr has, at least five years of study before he can be anointed, but he is very likely to succeed Sistani as the Iraqi Ayatollah, when Sistani dies, or if, at the time, Sadr gives him a little help into the Great Beyond."

Bis looked at his Corporal, with a doubtful eye, wondering if he should accept all of this second hand intelligence, but admitting, "If all this should come to pass, Sadr, at thirty-five or so, would be one of the youngest Ayatollahs," adding, "That should give Bush II, Israel, and Petraeus pause to reflect."

Before Tooley could answer, the radio blared forth with the voice of the Bradley sergeant saying, "The engineers should be here in a few minutes. They had to go the long way around, as their lead truck got road bombed. They lost the driver and wounded two," adding, "I told them both our unit and yours will give them ample cover when they arrive. Aim your carbines on the rubble and buildings north of Qud Street. That should hold their heads down."

"Gear up, guys," Bis ordered, "We move out in a few minutes. Wait for my order. As we deploy from the Stryker, I will be ahead of you. I will point to the position I want each of you to take, as each of the Bradley guys vacate," adding, "Anyone who strikes out on his own will rue the day, from me."

Bis moved to the back of the vehicle, near the ramp, telling the driver, "Wait for my signal before you open up."

"I hope all this effort has a happy ending," one of the squadsman declared.

Another squadsman replied, "You want a happy ending. IT depends on who writes the story, and where the story stops."

The first squadsman retorted, "Well one thing is certain, nobody on this Stryker wrote the story."

"Nobody in the 711th Brigade or in the US Military in Iraq either," Bis said to himself, *"The story comes straight out of the minds of Bush II, and his handlers, and so far it is a tragedy equal to anything Shakespeare ever wrote."*

Chapter VI – The Patriot

The Tigris River isn't the same as the Des Moines River, which had attracted to its green banks, Ian Otto von Bismarck, back in Iowa, but it was moving water.

There was no need to try to fish, as in the Iowa River, because there are not any edible fish. If there were, the upstream Iraqis would have extricated them miles ago.

Just to sit on an available river bank, like the Tigris provided to Bis' Green Zone existence, gave him some solitude, quietude, and a "get away from it all" change. He found it a good way to revitalize himself.

Bis watched the mesmerizing flowing water, as he leaned back in the welcome shade provided by an adjacent building. He involuntarily found himself daydreaming. He remembered this same Tigris River, as it was back in September of 2003 when, as a lowly private in the Iowa National Guard, he was part of the Bush-Cheney-Wolfowitz-Feith invasion team, eager to free the Iraqi people from the shackles of the world despised Saddam Hussein, and the United States from a fatal destruction by Saddam's weapons of mass destruction.

The appearance of the Tigris, and the Green Zone, was much different then. Both were full of debris from the American invasion, and the aftermath of the Iraqi people's unreasonable resistance. *"Not the Iraqi Army,"* Bis laughingly thought, *"but the fight in the Iraqi people, including both the Sunni and Shi'ite. This did not jive with the briefings we got from the army brass back at Camp Shelby, Mississippi. This was where the 3rd Squadron of the 221st Cavalry, Iowa National Guard, Ian's military group, out of Camp Dodge, at Des Moines, Iowa, were trained for their probable Middle East deployment."*

Continuing his daydreams, Bis remembered the glowing words, *"Iraqi people will probably shower you with flowers,"* adding, *"Some flowers. They were spiked with reconstituted artillery shells. They did,"* Bis concluded, *"make an avid impression on all concerned."*

Lapsing into serious thoughts, Bis then recalled how he learned about the Muslim plane hijackings on September 11, 2001, *"I, like most Americans, got my news from the cable and network television news programs. I did not rationalize beyond that. I was busy as an associate professor of English Literature, trying to obtain tenure at a small, Episcopalian, private college called Grannell, located at Grannell, Iowa, a few miles north of Des Moines, Iowa."*

Bis continued to recall, *"Like everyone else, as a patriotic American, I was shocked that a motley bunch of Muslims could hijack several American commercial airliners with such ease, and crash them into a New York skyscraper, killing themselves, all the passengers, and four thousand people located in the building.*

"Like most Americans, I had no idea of what constituted the Islamic faith. What was a book called the Koran? What was a Sunni? A Shi'ite? What motivated Muslim hijackers to commit suicide? Which Middle East country did they come from? The answers to these questions were not part of my learning process, nor that of most Americans.

"What gullible fools we all were," Bis thought. *"The* Weekly Standard *and all the other neo-con press told us the hijackers were a product of Saddam Hussein's dictatorial madness, and that only an invasion of Iraq would keep America safe.*

"There I was," Bis meditated, *"a 1995 honors graduate from St. Paul Lutheran College. Top man in my English Literature major. Supposedly a well educated American,"* laughing, *"I was so easily deceived from the real truth that the Muslim hijackers were actually citizens of Saudi Arabia. That they were Sunni Muslims, long-standing enemies of Saddam, and were the products of a branch of Sunni Muslim instruction called Wauhobism, financed both in Saudi Arabia, and in Moslem mosques in America, by Saudi Arabian royalty, our supposed friend and ally.*

"I was even fooled," Bis remembered, *"that Iraq was loaded with military bases and warehouses, filled with nuclear weapons of mass destruction, to*

be rained down on the United States," he chuckled, "*when Saddam had no planes or missiles capable of carrying, nor, in fact, any nuclear, or other weapons of mass destruction left in Iraq, after Israeli bombers, months before 9-11, had destroyed what little nuclear capability he did have.*

"*But,*" he thought, "*so were seventy-five percent of the American people. I did not really start looking into the truth until I got back to Iowa, from my first Iraqi tour in September of 2004.*"

Bis got up, picked up a small rock, juggled it a bit, and then threw it into the Tigris, a bit of self depreciation, then thinking, "*I knew so much about George Washington, and Nathan Hale from my mother's teaching, but little about the Middle East world, except what came out of the neo-cons' Israel, and the liberal news programs.*" Bis re-sitting further on down, in the shade of another adjacent building, blamed, not only himself, but also the administrators and the education majors who ran his high school, and also ran his college History and Social Studies. "*They,*" he remembered, "*dwelled on one worldism, and share America with Africa and Asia, and other anti-self dependence ideas. His books and teachers suggested, instead, an intentional socialist agenda, which was designed to promote consumerism, prolificacy, sexual looseness, and government dependency, rather than the old Christian virtues of frugality, thrift, responsibility, and self reliance.*"

Bis, throwing another stone into the Tigris, began returning back to his barracks, thinking, "*I had joined the 221ˢᵗ Cavalry Unit, of the Iowa Guard, solely as a patriotic duty, back in June of 2002, and was fully supported in doing so, by all the staff, and the administration of Grannell College.*

"*The undivided support of Grannell,*" his thinking continued, "*quickly diminished after his return from Iraq, from his first tour in September of 2004. It was then that he began looking for the truth about Iraq and the pro-invasion attitude, which controlled the Bush II Administration. Various irrefutable writings and publications were found, several of which were available to all Americans, but for many reasons were ignored. They clearly provided damning evidence of non-Saddam involvement in 9-11. The continuing Bush II bashing of Syria and Iran, after 9-11, were also discredited by several American intelligence agencies, and other American government official reports. It seems the media and Bush II had covered up the fact that Syria and Iran had both offered, without conditions, to assist in the fight against al-Qaeda. I already was aware the military had found that Saddam had no weapons of mass destruction capabilities, by my personal observation, general knowledge, and by talking with various military officers, while I was in Iraq.*"

Bis passing the PX, got a cup of coffee and a sandwich, and, while eating this semi feast at a small table, continued to remember, thinking, "*How unfortunate it is for our American culture that so many of its citizens have, and continued to have, such a massive public self-inflicted ignorance about what is so important to guarantee American survival in this modern world. The facts clearly show American citizens are continuously lied to, deceived, improperly taxed, and intentionally considered fly-bys and idiots by the elites, who, then constantly mock them. This deception is mostly by the media, but it also includes the several politicians they blindly re-elect every two, four, and six years. It exceeds amazement. It borders on insanity."*

Bis remembered relating his newly found facts to some of the professional staff, and sundry others, at Grannell, letting loose with his displeasure at various coffee breaks, and at other official college functions. The truth of what he said was like a lead balloon, laughing to himself, *"If I had not been notified by the Pentagon that our Iowa Guard Unit, the 221st Cavalry, was going to be recalled to Iraq for their second tour of duty, in December of 2005, the college administrators might have found some way to remove me from the teaching staff at Grannell."* Bis also remembered a similar Pentagon notification, at the same time, which related, from here on out, the various Guard Units would be deployed in Iraq for fifteen months, and then be allowed to come home for only twelve months, before being re-deployed. *"I considered myself better off than most of the guys in my 3rd Squadron. I had just been promoted to a three striper Sergeant, and my enlistment in the Guard expired in 2006. I felt sorry for most of the married guys, whose families were put under a tremendous stress. The only stress I felt, was the obvious anxiousness of the Grannell College administration to see me safely, or even unsafely, off to Iraq,"* he chuckled, also recalling, *"The army had initiated a 'stop loss' policy, which prevented soldiers from leaving any military service until three months after their Unit returned from Iraq,"* so he reasoned, *"I would not be able to leave my Guard Unit, legally, until fifteen months, plus three more months had gone by, dating from the December 2005 deployment."*

Bis, recalling his earlier extensive self-study of American History, and recognizing the sacrifices made by the several American heroes he read about, and admired, began thinking, *"The usual American citizen, now-a-days, has become soft, uncaring, and ignorant. He has become too much in love with himself, and with the material things, and liberal actions that gratify him. He has become addicted to government handouts, and emoluments. He no longer is self reliant, nor is he willing to take chances, and if he does, and fails, he looks to the politicians to rescue him."*

Strolling over to the waste container, he threw in it his empty coffee cup and sandwich cover, and continued the walk back to his barracks, thinking, *"Hold on. I can't equate today's normal citizens, with citizens that existed in America's earlier history. Those were different times, and different economies. Sound money, a healthy agriculture, and thriving manufacturing bases, were prospering back then, along with being able to obtain a practical, true learning, locally controlled education. Plus there was a community mentality requiring virtue, policed by the people's normal Christian attitudes and their demeanor.*

"Today's Americans, in order to find work, are largely concentrated into gang bothered, crowded cities, forced to work in big box stores, assembly lines, or

cubicles created by multi-national elite corporations, which have no respect for, what used to be, the coveted middle class, American worker, and whose corporate bosses will sacrifice just about anything, including their country, and their own honor, for money, even the fast depreciating only paper American dollar.

"*A big percentage of present American citizens have no father, and many so-called families are merely people who happen to live together,*" Bis reasoned. "*It is no wonder that the elites, and the liberal media, are able to get away with their obvious lies, and deceits, especially, when they are also able to bring in millions of illegal, low wage earning Mexicans, and legal, but low wage earning Indian technicians, intentionally to compete with, what remains of the old middle class.*

"*Its hard to conceive,*" Bis thought, "*that these same middle class Americans, now being bankrupted by their own government, and the money grubbing elite, multi-national American corporations, were once the controlling political voice in America.*

"*Still,*" he thought, ambling over to sit down on an ammunition crate, "*There are millions of American citizens, who have not been compromised by government handouts. Who have, through it all, been able to retain normal, probably mostly Christian families. Who desperately want to maintain the America of old, but don't know where to start, or what to do.*"

Bis reflected on that set of facts for a few minutes, and then concluded, "*Neither do I. To publicly challenge the elites, the neo-con media, and the liberal politicians is to invite being attacked personally, as a racist, anti-Jewish, anti-free trade, and any other disparaging adjective. I returned back to Grannell from my second Iraqi tour, and it is typical of what can happen, even though I kept a somewhat low profile. Within six months, the Grannell administration found ways to deny me tenure, and were not going to renew my teaching contract.*

"The media and the elite are easily able to maintain their total control by this vicious personal attack method. Few citizens can withstand such a blistering barrage.

"How can America be regenerated?" Bis pondered. *"The Christian religion must be involved somehow, but how? Many Christians are unorganizable. Many truly believe in some liberal things beyond Christianity. Many consider government handouts only as charitable. Many other semi-Christians have allowed their Christian beliefs to degenerate into only a 'good feeling' phenomenon."*

Bis stood, paced a few steps, and returned to his ammunition crate chair, thinking, *"Christianity is, basically, a way of life, directed by God, the only God, and requires faith only in Him. For skeptics, God not only gave us His Son, Jesus Christ, but provided unassailable witnesses to God's miracles, in Jesus, the disciples,, the apostles, and the thousands who witnessed events that could only be orchestrated by God. The underlying principles of Christianity must be applied, but neither the individual churches, nor the various Christian denominations can officially be in charge. There must be an overwhelming voluntary desire, on the part of Christian America, to reject statism. America, at its historic best, not only was*

"I should Court Martial your Brigade Sergeant," Bis countered, offering an obviously displeased, serious face, "He has no military business looking into my official records, nor publicizing them."

Tooley immediately paled, saying, "I thought you would be amused. I'm sorry. I got that information because I have a special relationship with the Brigade Sergeant. I have not told anyone else. I swear."

Bis, hearing that, softened up, commenting, "Its not that I object to either relationship. What I don't want is what you did, mimicking the Prussian Military mindset, which then goes from bad to worse." He continued, "I then get the same old Otto quotations, as, 'There is a special providence that protects idiots, drunkards, children and the United States of America.'"

"I understand," Tooley responded, "like his advice about making laws is like making sausage. It will remain our secret."

The Corporal continued, "But it is also common knowledge that you were an English Literature Professor before you became a regular army, elite forces, Stryker First Sergeant. I am curious as to how that came about."

"A combination of my patriotic love for America, and my relish in working with the common, ordinary, dog-faced American GI's. It was all tied to an effort to compensate for the loss of my professor's title, as a direct result of my abandonment of political correctness."

The Corporal, wanting to hear more, leaned up against the wall in Bis' semi-private room, refusing to leave. Bis, reluctantly, sat down on his footlocker to remove his boots, and then related to Tooley, "You are aware that I still think our misadventure in Iraq has been a horrendous, maybe even fatal, strategic mistake. If I were commander, I would immediately pull all US troops out of this self imposed, anti-Christian, Moslem induced holocaust."

He continued, "I returned to my English Literature classes with relish, after my second Iraqi tour, in March of 2007. At a low key, I reiterated my concerns to the staff about where Bush II, and his neo-cons were taking America, and wondered why the media and the universities were not taking up the obvious, unchallenged destruction of our culture. I was met with immediate hostility at what I thought was a center of learning's job. I was no longer welcome at Grannell College functions, or at its Staff Meetings. Even though it was an Episcopal college, they were abhorred at my mere mentioning that the media and religious colleges were not only, not protesting what was their basic function, but actually were aiding and abetting the ongoing Christian bashing.

"My expiring enlistment in the Iowa Guard happened to come up during that same time in 2007," Bis continued. "It coincided with Grannell's efforts to cause me to be fired. Providence, in the form of an army recruitment officer, appeared that same summer, informing me about the advantages I would fall heir to, for an additional six year enlistment. This time, however, not as a guardsman, but as a sergeant in the Green Berets, or the Rangers, or possibly with a new elite group of Brigades the Army was forming, called the Strykers. I was offered, as a special inducement, a cash bonus, plus special duty pay of three hundred seventy-five dollars per month, over and above my normal pay, a special offer given only to first sergeants and master sergeants. They told me it was to keep people like me from being hired by private security companies. The State Department gives big bucks for these guys to protect them in Iraq, kind of like a personal bodyguard."

"The military is having troubles keeping quality volunteers," offered the Corporal, "Especially with the new, extended tours in Iraq. The Brigade Sergeant told me that fifty percent of the captains and majors who recently graduated from West Point are leaving the service. Also, that only three in ten of the new recruits brought in can really meet the military's health, educational, and moral standards."

"The problem is deeper than that," Bis disclosed. "The current Iraqi demand for the army exceeds the supply. The Iraq War has so depleted our Armed Forces, to such an extent, we would have no ready strategic reserve to protect American interests if another crisis, such as a belligerent China, would arise."

"Iraq was also wearing out the army's war making machinery," Tooley claimed. "The Guard Units are really taking it on the nose. Their equipment, now being used in Iraq, is eroding from use, or being destroyed, and is un-repairable, but it is also not being replaced, and Units returning home are therefore handicapped in handling local incidents."

"That was another reason I signed up for six more years," Bis confessed. "The political pressure to pull out of Iraq is causing the Pentagon to depend, more and more, on Special Operation Forces. They need a smaller military force that can perform small scale raids, long range reconnaissance and other secretive operations, with a better than even chance of getting it done."

Bis continued, "That's where the Strykers come in. My re-enlistment was at a time when Rumsfeld was restructuring the old, Cold War American Army into one which could adapt to more unconventional warfare, such as the use of roadside bombs."

"Using the term, 'IMPROVISED EXPLOSIVE DEVICES,' in Iraq," the Corporal interrupted, "had to be devised by a Staff Officer," laughing, "A GI would have called it 'a doctored up artillery shell'."

"The Pentagon, as a result," Bis continued, "set up, what they called 'Future Combat Systems' or as we call them, 'Brigade Combat Teams'."

"I agree that the Army's MI-Abrams tank is older than our GI's," Tooley countered. "I don't think they should be discarded, as long as Red China is around, we might need them."

Bis smiled, nodded, and continued, "That is why Rumsfeld authorized the creation of forty-three new mobile brigade oriented units to eventually replace the, then in use, heavy divisions. At the time I re-enlisted, the Pentagon was deploying sergeants like me, not only in Berets, and Rangers, but because I was willing to train as a new Stryker Squadron Commander, I would be placed in one of the developing Stryker

Brigades then being formed. The first Stryker, already trained from the Army's 3rd Infantry Division, was then operational in Iraq. Incidentally, I also was guaranteed two rocker stripes to go along with my existing three stripes."

"That always helps," Tooley commented. "Did you train together with the present Squadron you now command? Since I was transferred to you, directly from an Intelligence Unit, after your Squadron got to Iraq, I don't really know the history."

"Except for you and two good men who were killed," Bis replied, "and two others who were transferred, I, and the rest of the 7th Squadron, have been together since the beginning. Our Brigade was deployed to Iraq in January of 2008."

Bis continued, "I'm not happy to be in Iraq, but I am happy with my Stryker outfit. It is a common sense solution to the new kind of warfare the Army finds itself in. Being wheeled makes it highly mobile, and although a Stryker costs four million dollars each, and draws some complaints that the .50 caliber machine guns arming the combat vehicle should be bigger, I have found them big enough. It will easily handle any enemy arms I am called on to go up against. It can carry soldiers the size of my Squadron without a problem. Being fast, and also capable of going through narrow streets and alleys, you put five or six of them together, and you have a highly maneuverable small army. The Moslems are tactically surprised. They don't expect such a force rumbling through their home towns, so soon."

Bis continued, "Its size also means many types of aircraft can transport it, and the top of the vehicle can be used for taking out wounded, fire support, and hauling in, or taking out, more troops as indicated."

"The officers like the Stryker," Tooley added, "because it has a unique reconnaissance, and networked communication capabilities, allowing Brigade officers to get real time reports from their troops, and to then issue orders quickly. The staff officers also like the fact that a Stryker, being wheeled, does not damage the road network, like a tank or halftrack does."

"The Stryker, bottom line, gives the Army a middle ground of capabilities," Bis responded. "Its framework, and the positioning of its armor, and other features also allow the Stryker to be easily upgraded with newer technology as it comes on the market."

"You do, however, present an unusual set of facts," Tooley contended, changing the subject. "I would bet that no other elite attack force has a squadron leader who also can recite Shakespeare."

"I doubt it would impress al-Sadr, or al-Maliki, for me to yell out, 'Out damn spot,' like Hamlet's mother screamed," adding, "It would not change those malignant Iraqi damned spots, or change this damn war one damn bit," Bis laughed.

"It would impress me," the Corporal commented. "I just pray both of us get back to an America, which also is impressed by such things as a Shakespeare set of beautiful words, safe and sound."

"You will find, in Iraq, as in America, 'Tomorrow and tomorrow, creeps on in this petty pace to the last syllable of recorded time,'" Bis, chuckling, again quoted Shakespeare in response to Tooley's prayer, "Tomorrow here will also be tomorrow there. The American people, tomorrow, as they have done before, will respond."

"Yeah," the Corporal replied, "but, like someone else said, 'In the long run, we're all dead.'"

"Our chances, in the long run, get less with each passing tomorrow, so tomorrow's chances might be a problem."

"There was once a brilliant Roman poet," Bis closed out the conversation, saying, "His name was Ovid. He pointed out, 'Chance is always powerful. Let your hook be always cast. In the pool where you least expect it, there will be a fish.'"

Chapter VIII –
Bis Lets Loose

Tuesday, June 10, 2008, after several days of no combat deployment, either in Sadr City, or other less lethal parts of Baghdad, Bis and his now confirmed, new corporal, used the down time to make sure the soldiers of their 7th Squadron were ready and able. Corporal Tooley, using his connections at Brigade, made sure the Squadron members had all the combat clothing and equipment available, along with plenty of cleaning kits, and spare parts for their M-4's.

Bis had the 7th Squadron's Stryker pulled into the Green Zone repair shop, a spot usually reserved for the General's and the State Department's Baghdad touring vehicles. Bis was one of a few able to have the chief mechanic and his assistant mechanics check over the 7th Squadron's combat weary Stryker. They did it as a favor for Bis, and as a mark of respect for him. The mechanics told Bis, "It's a good thing. We found several circuits that, if they had not been replaced, could have proved disastrous in a combat situation."

As Bis and his driver brought the refurbished, but still bullet nicked, Stryker back to its normal Green Zone parking area, Bis' driver commented, "She might have a few bullet holes, and need a new paint job, but she drives and operates just as good as the day she came off the factory's production line."

It was just at that time, unexpectedly, three private SUV, four-wheel drives, wheeled by Bis, each SUV containing four private security contractors on board. The private bodyguards had on ball caps, some backwards, sun glasses, full beards, and each clutching an AK-47.

"There goes some ham and eggers, loaded with guns. Odd that nobody is ever around controlling them," the driver interposed.

"Yeah," Bis responded. "I see them all the time, tooling around Baghdad, supposedly bodyguarding State Department, some Department of Defense, personnel, and visiting congressmen."

"They tell me," the driver replied, "there are fifty thousand of them in Iraq, knocking down fifty to seventy-five thousand a year. Beats a PFC's pay."

He continued, "They used to be mostly ex-Seals and Berets and Rangers, and were more self-disciplining then. They looked good, and got lots of GI respect. Now, most of them are considered no account profit seekers and Third World commandoes."

The two parked their Stryker. Bis, curious about the bodyguards, decided to stop by the office of a State Department young lady he had become acquainted with. Facts about these ham and eggers might be forthcoming through this friend who worked there, and in whom he had more than a passing interest.

Excusing himself, from the driver, Bis walked unnoticed into the young lady's office, giving Bis the romantic opportunity to place both hands gently over her eyes. It quickly brought her response, "Sergeant, be careful, the State Department has eyes in the front and in the back of its head. Unfortunately," she giggled, "neither seems to see straight."

"How did you know it was me?" Bis demanded.

"You are the only one with the guts to do it," she answered, "Besides; I saw your GI sleeves. They gave you away.

"You always have a good reason," she continued, "What can I do for you?"

"I'm curious about all these private bodyguards," Bis responded. "Can you give me some details about them?"

"Going to run for office, huh," the lady commented, laughing. "I can give you plenty of facts," as she opened a drawer in her desk, using a key she took from her purse, admitting, "I would only do this for you."

She pulled out a card file, and thumbing through the cards, commented, "There are approximately one hundred eighty thousand private contractors in Iraq at this time. Only about sixty thousand could be described as you're curious about armed bodyguards. Blackwater, being the main, longtime contractor, has received over one billion dollars, since the Iraq War started."

Bis shook his head in disbelief, asking, "How did this boondoggle all get started, this business of trading private mercenaries for the US Army?"

"Its legal beginning is congressionally called, the Army's Logistics Civil Augmentation Program," she replied. "Its funding is open-ended, and it is an inspiring cost plus. The first big bite for the private contractors came from Dick Cheney, when he was Secretary of Defense under Bush I. He was able to talk Congress into appropriating four billion dollars under the program. The first big bucks went to a firm called Brown and Root. When Cheney left the Defense office, becoming the private CEO of Halliburton in 1995, it just so happened, Halliburton happened to be the parent company of Brown and Root."

"Shame on Cheney. Shame on Congress," Bis declared.

"You think that's bad," the young lady commented, "A bigger tragedy occurred when Paul Bremer was appointed the head of Iraq's 'Coalition Provisional Authority,' by Douglas Feith and Paul Wolfowitz back in 2004. Bremer hired Blackwater personal bodyguards, to the tune of twenty-one million dollars. Wherever he went in Iraq, he was always surrounded by thirty-six civilian guards, which used up a complete motor pool of SUV's. He also had two bomb sniffing dogs, four private pilots, along with four aerial gunners, and three private Boeing MD-530 helicopters."Bis, his eyes raised by these facts, interposed, "He obviously did not trust the military. Under the circumstances, I can see why," adding, "How many contractors are in Iraq today?"

"The present count is seven thousand three hundred security contractors working for the Defense Department. One thousand in Afghanistan, and two thousand five hundred work for my boss, the State Department," she responded.

Bis smiled, and winking, said, "Thank you Sweetheart. Let me know if I can do you a favor."

She smiled and said nothing, but her eyes wrote a two volume set.

Giving the attractive young lady another smile, Bis was about to further comment, when her State Department boss came, unexpectedly, into her office. He gave Bis a terse, unless you have important business, get your butt out of here, look.

Bis said nothing, wanting not to create problems, and gave the lady a salute, as he walked out the office door.

The Brigade's Staff Office was located between State and Bis' barracks, and he decided to make a stop there to pick up any orders, mail, or other communications deposited in the box posted for the 7th Squadron. While he was thumbing through the communications, a staff officer, a major, who took a liking to Bis, came through the door, going to his office. He had, on occasion, talked to Bis, during the few short months the 7th Squadron had been in Iraq. He had recognized Bis' obvious leadership qualities, and had offered to sponsor Bis into taking an Officer's Candidate School slot, when next they came up.

"Come in my office," said the Major, "I'd like to get your opinions on a few things."

When a major invites you, you accept, Bis realized, but he also liked the Major, and wanting his opinion, asked him, "What do you think of all these private contractors around here, particularly the ones acting as bodyguards?"

The Major smiled, and then commented, "Not very much. They cost the taxpayers a whole bunch, and they get in the way of the Army. They are a hindrance rather than a help."

The Major continued, "With Sadr shooting up the Green Zone using reconstituted artillery, we also have had to commit combat troops, we don't have, to protect them, both here and in the so-called 'International Zone', where they, and the media congregate, in central Baghdad," adding, "But since the big wigs use them for ego trips, they are likely to remain."

"I noticed them donning body armor, Kevlar jackets," Bis replied. "I even heard one contractor admitting that he moved his desk to an area where he thought it would deflect shrapnel, as if that would make any difference."

The Major nodded, then picking up a paper, and looking for an answer, interposed, "I want to get a GI's opinion, your opinion, on what the Army should do about Emir Muqtada al-Sadr, and his Shi'ite Mahdi Militia."

"Army, don't you mean," Bis responded, "I think Sadr's position was stated very clearly when he made a speech, and later executed a Fatwa, or Emir edict, a few weeks ago, saying, 'The time has come to express your rejections and raise your voices loud against the unjust Occupier and enemy of nations and humanity, and against the horrible massacres committed by the Occupier against our honorable people,'" adding, "Sadr's position is uncompromising. He always calls and obviously considers the US Army as the 'Occupier'.

Bis continued, "I'm going to give you my honest opinions, and I know, if they should become general knowledge to the generals now running Iraq, they would ship me not only out of the Army, but also Iraq, and if they could, America. I think it will not change. Bush II people, and his Petraeus type generals, are intentionally lying, or else smoking something illegal, when they tell America, over and over again, that we are making great progress in Iraq. They promise, 'Just wait a few more months,' which ultimately turns into years, inflicting more American GI deaths in this endless, useless, turmoil," adding, "They, for some irrational reason, want to satisfy the neo-cons, and the Israeli general staff, who mistakenly think that Iraq will, suddenly, emerge as a meek, Israeli loving Islamic democracy. Believing Iraq will welcome with open arms, the elite neo-cons, inviting them to come, drill their oil, and offering to buy their cheap, Chinese made, outsourced commercial junk."

Bis cautioned, "I think a lot of you Major, and I trust you. Otherwise, I would not be so forthcoming. We both are aware, just a few days ago, the American generals fell all over themselves, as to who could apologize first, and quickest, to the anti-American, anti-Christian Sadrites, along with the Hussein loving Sunnis. It was because it was made public that an American sharp shooter had used the Moslem 'Book

Bis suddenly stopped, looked over at the Major, and said, "I'm sorry. I'm ranting on. I'm sure you have other things to do."

The Major responded, "On the contrary. Please continue. This is a side I find very interesting."

Bis, involuntarily, shifted in his chair, and then continued, "The big changes in America can be traced to the time of the Great Depression of the 1930's, the Second World War, and the political dominance for forty years of the Democrats, running almost unopposed with their socialist, and big government ideas. The Democrats were aided and abetted by an alliance with several big government Republicans in the Congress, and leaders such as Ford. Their alliance, and dominance, caused a great transformation in America.

"The former Christian virtues of frugality, small government, savings, self-sufficiency, and moral strictness, were chipped away by a new type American. An elite American, who, with the help of a kept media, lobbyist kept politicians, and the appearance of fast track computers, arose and almost single handedly changed the American goals from living a happy, satisfying life, to a life where Americans were baited by consumerism, and an anything goes mentality. At the same time, it was bankrupting the Middle Class; it was giving unjust riches to the instigating elites.

"These culture controlling elite citizens found enormous riches, not just in the millions, but in the billions. The use of newly found instant communications, along with the aid of the co-conspiring media and supportive politicians, allowed these elites, to create a giant Las Vegas out of, what used to be, America."

Bis continued, "Most of these new elites are basically speculators, and do not actually produce anything useful, except as it might arise incidentally from multi-national corporations, who by outsourcing labor to Red China realize huge profits. These speculator's offices are staffed only with all the new communication gadgets, secretaries, and a stable of lobbyist-lawyers, whose jobs are to keep track of the tax laws, but mainly to lobby and bribe politicians, in supporting the elitists' loose activities."

Bis stopped, fixed his eyes on the Major, who, with obvious gestures, urged the Sergeant to continue.

Bis again shifted his legs, then proceeded with his unorthodox commentary, "The speculation of these elites, big time gamblers, is extracting billions from the Middle Class, and from the nation's other money sources, which necessarily at the same time, reduces those entities to a poverty like status.

"These elites," Bis continued, "are essentially placing bets, using the computerized world markets, as to whether or not, oil or grain or whatever, is going up or down, whether the dollar, or the Euro, is dropping or rising, and betting on the upraise, or the downturn, of a thousand other market manipulable items. The only value the elites produce is ciphers in their own bank accounts," laughing, "But only a paper value, the real soundness of which can be argued, after Richard Nixon took America off the Gold Standard," adding, "But the elites' interference in the world markets, cause huge price variations, which reflect something other than the market measured, supply and demand, which establish a usual true value."

"Many economists insist that these speculators are only part of the free market system," the Major interposed, "What do you say to that?"

"That is the theory," Bis replied, "Some of those economists try to sell that erroneous theory, based on their contention that putting billions of dollars in the pockets of a few elite speculators will, somehow, cause people to use less of the oil, or grain, or whatever, but whose price has been caused to rise because of their speculation, not the actions of the market?"

Bis continued, "For the price to reflect a true free market value, only those things which are actually necessary in the production of grain or oil, such as the cost of seed, or the cost of drilling, the cost of planting and harvesting, or the cost of refining, the transportation of both to the wholesaler, and retailer."

Bis stopped, and looking at the Major, challenged him, "You tell me, where, in any of those processes, the elite spectator is a necessity."

The Major shook his head and remained speechless.

"Our elite speculator only adds, big time, to the top of those costs," Bis declared, "But it is this total inflated cost, which our Middle Class American is forced to pay in the end."

Bis shifted one last time in his chair, explaining to the Major, "I have been wanting to get these facts off my mind and chest, for a long time. I appreciate your acting as my sounding board. I am going to bend your ear one more time in my plea to enlist your help in extricating our troops out of this god-forsaken Muslim trap, which trap America has materially helped the Emirs to set, to comically and tragically catch itself. It is a kind of death wish, a contagious disease.

"I am also aware," Bis proceeded, introducing a new subject, "and I am sure that you are also aware, although it has not been made public, that our esteemed Iraqi Ayatollah Sistani has quietly informed his Shi'ite followers that they should continue their armed protests against the American troops now occupying Iraq. Although Sistani is eighty-years-old, he evidently wants to remain the Ayatollah. It is mainly a defensive movement, on his part, to thwart the Sadr Mahdi Army's successes. The majority of Iraqi citizens, however, agree wholeheartedly."

The Major nodded, commenting, "Sistani's actions have put a real kink in Bush's Iraq Policy, which assumes Sistani as a Maliki ally," adding, Maliki has also become a big, unexpected stumbling block. He has failed to get the Iraqi Parliament to approve, not only a renewal of the usual 'Status of Forces' Agreement, which the US has with every nation in which it has troops, but also a vital 'Strategic Framework Agreement', which is essential, if the US is to legally remain as a peaceful force, under its authorizing original UN mandate in Iraq."

"I don't know how many of these clear, 'We don't want anything to do with you' statements the Shi'ite leaders, and the Emirs have to make, to insure that Bush and company will get it through their thick heads, that there will not be a peaceful bilateral security agreement, for one hundred years, or for one year, between the US, and Maliki's Iraq. Such a pact, allowing American troops to remain in the area, is mainly to protect Israel's interests. The US is viewed as only a military occupier, and not as an Iraqi helpmate, or an ally, as Petraeus would have us believe. If US troops, all one hundred fifty thousand of them, remain in Iraq, it will not be by the agreement of the Iraqi people, either Sunni or Shi'ite, both of which have an intense hatred of any occupier. It will only be possible by the force of arms."

"If that happens," echoed the Major, "This ongoing, never-ending, brutal guerilla war, with its ever increasing American casualties, will finally engender an overwhelming intense desire for stopping this death wish war, by the American people. The Iraq War will not be supported."

Bis stood. He pulled himself up to full attention. He saluted the Major, sharply, saying, as he walked out of his office, "The opinions of American GI's, and those of non-general officers, are surprisingly similar. The truth cannot avoid being the truth, except when politics are involved."

Chapter IX –
Father's Day

Sunday, June 15, 2008, dawned without the 7th Squadron of the 7th Stryker Cavalry Regiment, 711th Stryker Brigade, for several days not being ordered to patrol various parts of Sadr City, indeed, not even Baghdad proper.

As Bis, and his corporal, breakfasted together in the Squadron's mess, Tooley reminded him, "It is Father's Day," asking, "I don't suppose you have any kids?"

Bis laughed out loud, saying, "You know I'm not married."

"That does not mean anything anymore," Tooley countered. "However, I'm not a father either, but we do have three Squad members who are married, and two with children."

"This is Sunday," Bis noted, "Church day. Give them Monday off from performing Squadron duties.

Tell them to write home and tell their kids that the military respects fatherhood."

"You are being overly facetious, Sergeant," teased Tooley, "Maybe you are suppressing your own desire for fatherhood."

Bis was about to tell Tooley to practice psychiatry on his own time, when a Squadsman hustled up to their table to announce, "A truck blew up in the northern part of Baghdad. It exploded right in the middle of a Shi'ite wedding party.

"The tractor-trailer truck must have been super loaded with shells, rockets, explosives, and grenades, because the force of the blast crumbled several nearby two-story buildings, buried cars under rubble, sheared off a corrugated steel roof and left a huge crater."

"When?" Bis asked.

"Just an hour ago," answered the Squadsman.

"They got no respect for Father's Day," Tooley commented.

"I'll say they don't," replied the Squadsman, they killed ten Iraqis, and wounded forty-five wedding by-standers. I'm sure many of them were fathers."

"Sounds like it happened in a Shi'ite part of Baghdad," Bis reasoned, "Could be a Sunni operation."

"I doubt it," Tooley interposed, "The Sunnis don't have that kind of finesse. I would bet it might be the work of the Shi'ite Tamim Tribe. General Keanne, who is one of Petraeus' advisors, has been talking directly with the Chief Emir of the Shi'ite Tamims, according to Brigade, plying them generously with US taxpayers' dollars to rat on the Sadr people," adding,

"This is what they did with the Sunnis. The Tamims obviously don't get along with Muqtada al-Sadr."

"Our generals wouldn't use bribes, would they?" Bis laughed, answering his own question, "Yes they would. They would do anything to counter Sadr," adding, "They want the Tamims to inform to Maliki, and to the US command, the location, strength, and armament of the Sadr militias. That strategy worked, at least for a while, with the Sunnis, but the money cost is huge, and, like the Sunnis, it probably won't last long."

"Looks like we might get orders to saddle up," Tooley suggested. "Should I alert the Squad?"

"Not yet," Bis replied. "Lets see how Petraeus responds to this obvious setback," adding, "A few days ago, the generals also denied that the Iraqi Grand Ayatollah Ali al-Sistani, had told his close Shi'ite associates, in a secret meeting that, 'It is permissible to make armed resistance to US occupying troops.'"

"Wow," Tooley exclaimed. "That really would be a change from what the generals are telling us," adding, "Sistani is usually quiet about anything which would affect al-Maliki's government."

"It could signify a big, big change in the Bush-Petraeus position in Iraq," Bis commented. "For one thing, it could preview an alliance between Sistani and Sadr to jointly approve attacks on US forces," adding, "But the bigger issue would be a failure to approve the joint, long term strategic plan, to provide the US with Iraqi bases, plus control of Iraq's air spaces, which Bush is counting on."

"Maliki must fear Sistani and Sadr, more than he fears Petraeus," Tooley interposed. "Do you think the generals with this confronting them, will increase US troop strength to Iraq, in numbers more than the 2007, so-called surge reinforcements?"

"The Pentagon had to re-deploy guard units from the home states early, to get up to the thirty thousand they used in the 2007 surge," Bis responded, "That well is dry," adding, "The only way could be a draft, but that is politically impossible."

"You don't think they will extend our tours, do you?" Tooley asked.

"When generals and politicians are faced with apolitical problems," Bis answered, "they always do what is politically correct. They would extend tours if they have to. The Petraeus vow to reduce troop strength from one hundred fifty-five thousand to one hundred forty thousand is now only a pipe dream."

"You are right, Sergeant," Tooley commented. "The 7th Stryker Squadron is not a viable political constituency. It is, right now, potentially, cannon fodder."

"A Maliki-American confrontation," cautioned Bis, "could throw everything into doubt. You and I better keep a close eye on our Squadron."

The Corporal nodded, saying, "You can't always trust the generals. I'll always remember Major General Jeffrey Hammond's immortal words, as he bowed in reverence to the Sunni Chiefs north of Baghdad, when he used for an example, that poor GI sniper, who was found to have used a Koran book as target practice, 'In a humble manner, I look into your eyes today and I say, please forgive me and my soldiers. It was nothing more than criminal behavior,'" adding, "Since when is shooting into a book a court martial offense?"

"Iraq, with its continuing lies, being unwinnable, and yet judged by the media as politically correct," Bis interposed, "It is destroying the American military, both its men and its equipment," adding, "It allows, in fact it necessitates, promoting, and a must bring to the Iraqi command, politically correct soldier-politicians to lead the American army. Soldiers who only hear the political siren, and agree to back up the politician's manipulation are given a hero's status."

Bis, pausing for a few moments, added, "General George Patton must be, not only rolling over, but spinning, in his grave."

Tooley laughed, and then commented, "I just hope we find another Patton if we ever have to fight a military colossus, like Red China, instead of a third rate guerrilla army like we have in Iraq."

"I think we should call a 7th Squadron meeting," Bis declared, "In fact, I'm going to order it tomorrow, Monday evening right after mess, and right here in our barracks. I want you, Corporal, to assist me in reporting what is happening, and likely to happen, with Maliki, Petraeus, and the, so-called, Strategic Alliance Agreement. I want my Squad to know the real truth, including the fact that the US Army is, operating in Iraq, only as the head of an international army, and under an authorizing United Nations' Resolution that automatically expires at the close of 2008."

Bis continued, "What happens then, and in between times, is stuff our Squad should be informed about."

"For another thing," the Corporal replied, "they should know that the army has a total of forty-three combat brigades, sixteen of which are currently in Iraq, one in Korea, two slated for Homeland Defense, and the rest, being re-put together after Iraqi tours, or unavailable. That the war, which America, at first won, in Afghanistan, in a month after September 11, 2001, and then left undefended, so that Iraq could be invaded in March of 2003, is going badly, and will need troops in short order. The US might find it necessary to transfer troops, like our 7th Squadron, to bolster the thirty-five thousand US Troops that are already there, but can only do so, on a one-for-one reduction in Iraq. This would affect our Squad, either way."

"That's true," Bis agreed, nodding, "Even the Pentagon's practice of cross leveling, which means going into guard units, which have already finished an Iraqi tour, and plucking out troops necessary to fill out a brigade," adding, "The brigades to fill out, just don't exist."

Bis continued, "I'm also going to inform them that, if they could, Bush II and Petraeus would attack Iran. It is probably in our overall favor that the Iraqi Defense Minister, of Maliki's un-sovereign, sovereign Iraq, with the urging and complete concurrence of Maliki, only a few days ago, at a meeting with top Iranian officials, told them, 'Iraq will not allow the country to be used for an attack on Iran,' and that Iraq will seek, 'more bilateral cooperation with Iran.'"

"It looks like there will be no agreements at all," Tooley commented, "Let alone any long term strategic alliance between Bush and the Maliki government covering a slate of political, diplomatic, economic, and cultural ties, at least while Bush is president," adding, "There is also a lot of congressional interest to approve any agreement, but Bush says that any such agreement does not need a congressional assent."

Bis chuckled, and then added, "I guess Bush figures that something this important should not be decided by a flyover, hinterlands, congress. Only important people, such as Bush, the neo-cons, and the Israeli general staff, should make these decisions."

"The sovereignty of the United States is not deemed to be important," Tooley interposed, adding, "Don't forget to include Dick Cheney on that list."

"Or that only the US Congress can appropriate the money necessary to underwrite any proposed agreement," Bis pointed out, laughing, "Maybe Bush and Maliki can assess the Israeli taxpayers to pay for it."

"Fat chance," the Corporal conceded. "But our Squad should be told that, if Bush is going to get any kind of face saving agreement from Maliki, Bush and associates, the US would have to concede too much prior Iraqi approval, as to any US troop operations inside Iraq's borders, and strict limits on US troops outside its borders," adding, "It makes one wonder why we're here, and why we came here in the first place."

Bis, nodding in agreement, added, "Our Squadron should also know that any such pact with Maliki, would affect, adversely, their legal status, on the issue of immunity. We, even as US soldiers, could be prosecuted by Sunni judges for attacking Sunnis and Shi'ite judges for attacking Shi'ites. It is an impossible situation."

"It also leaves US contractors, and US government personnel in Iraq, open to prosecution," Bis concluded, thinking to himself, he also was going to warn his lady friend at the State Department office.

As Bis and Tooley got up from their breakfast table, Bis warned, "Maybe you don't want to be part of our Squad get together tomorrow night. We could be treated the same as that discredited sniper, if the wrong officers find out about the subject matter of our meeting."

Laughing, Tooley responded, "I would welcome it, especially since today's big truck explosion in Baghdad, plus Sadr's daily street demonstrations against any strategic alliance pact," adding, "I can also guarantee that our 7th Squadron, to a man, will not bad mouth anything we divulge to them tomorrow night."

Bis smiled, ending the long conversation with, "Have a happy future Father's Day. May you have many."

CHAPTER X –
THE GREEN ZONE
TOWN MEETING

"Welcome to the first, of the Seventh Squadron's Town Meetings," Tooley shouted out to his fellow squadsmen, a group of seven, head shaven, physically fit young Americans, from all sections of America, sitting in a row of fold down chairs, and all having a look of wonderment about what was going on.

"The first thing we are going to do," continued the Corporal, "is stand at attention, and salute Sergeant Bis, when I call him into the room," adding, "I know you don't have to salute sergeants, but I got a feeling you guys will agree to do that, as a sort of tribute."

Without waiting for an answer, Tooley walked back to Bis' semi-private room in the barracks, telling him, "The men are ready."

Bis then emerged from his quarters, and as he walked toward his men, he watched, in amazement as they, without a command, all rose to attention,

plantations they have created to put the rest of us on, will be difficult to leave."

"It is the fault of the Congress, and the bureaucrats," Tooley interjected. "Through political campaign donations, the elites have made congressmen their lap dogs," adding, "With all their money, the elites have also established ownership, control, and direction of most of the mainline media, including the printed, the networks, and cable, which, dutifully, tell the American people only what the elites want told them."

"I agree," the squadsman from Mobile responded. "What can we do about it?"

"First, the American middle class must inform themselves, or be informed of the truth about a matter," Tooley replied. "The concept of 'free trade' sounds so good on paper, but it is not. The middle class must defeat those congressmen who support it. It is really not free trade at all, but only provides subsides to those who want to destroy America. So-called free trade has taken at least twenty million jobs from America's middle class.

"Cultural Americans must insist that Congress enact tariffs and equalizing taxes on foreign imports. Americas can, and must, look to the internet, which is still allowed to express the truth, and an opinion, and also to non-governmental groups, formed to help preserve America and the middle class."

Bis stood up from his chair, during the interchange, and warned, "Remember, it is more important to preserve our unique American culture, than it is to find a Chinese made T-shirt at Wal-Mart, which is a dollar cheaper than the one made in America," adding, "That dollar might be the most important one you never spent."

"Congress has abandoned its sworn duty," Tooley commented. "They complain of a loss of civil rights, but fail to protect middle America in their loss of constitutional rights, most of which are embedded in the Bill of Rights."

Tooley continued, "A lot of our problems can be traced to the Congress, who has let the elites set the value of the dollar. The Constitution clearly gives Congress the power to coin money, and to regulate its value. They inexplicably turned that power over to a bunch of bankers, and named the prestigious give-away the 'Federal Reserve' back in Woodrow Wilson's day," adding, "Predictably, those controlling bankers have created a situation where they were allowed to make billions , by allowing sub-prime mortgages on unqualified, high interest paying borrowers. When they began losing money on the unqualified loans, the Federal Reserve bailed out the bankers with billion dollar loans of the taxpayers' money."

Bis stood again, at the disclosure, and warned, "Congress must take back its constitutional duty to restore American sound money. It should reinstate the Gold Standard. The useless Federal Reserve must be fired by the taxpayers," adding, "By supporting the unsupportable politics of the Federal Reserve, Congress has practically destroyed our once unexcelled agricultural and manufacturing base. We have become merely a service and information nation in the world, and most of that is now farmed out to India."

Bis concluded, "America must return to 'populism', which is control by the people in the middle. It is the middle who, previously, provided the money, the manpower, the material, and the productive incentives that made, and still makes, America work, and which, when allowed, bestows money blessings on all, rather than an elitist few."

Another squadsman, single, never married, who hailed from Indiana, commented, "I think a lot of the money problem evolves from the failure of the media, and I mean all of them, who hide information from Americans. They bury those people who are trying to warn them of what bad money can do. Look at the Republican candidate, Ron Paul. He has, essentially, been filtered out of the media's news cycle, and has been, for the several months, so far, of the 2008 Presidential Campaign," adding, "We all know this is happening. My question is why? What can be done about it?"

Corporal Tooley framed an answer to the Indianan's question, saying, "The biggest reason is because the media is owned and controlled by the same elites who profit from a 'Fiat' currency, which the dollar has become. These elites would support either the Democrat, or the Republican, which are now in the forefront, as neither has campaigned as supporting sound money," adding, "The Republican Party has been strangely silent about the treatment given one of their candidates, but the Republicans are not the party I knew when I was growing up."

The Indianan nodded, and then interposed, "The neo-cons now completely control the Republican Party."

Bis again stood and commented, "As bad as the complete suffocation of any mention of Ron Paul by the media is, the bigger problem for America lies again with both of the political parties, and the media. It is their promotion of government programs, which favor one class of Americans over another, and the taxing of one set of Americans at a different rate than another set of Americans," adding, "Nothing will destroy a nation's solidarity quicker. It inevitably pits some Americans against other Americans."

Bis continued, "Ronald Reagan's presidency was successful because he cut the tax rates of all Americans equally. The result was the resurrection of the American economy from the Carter doldrums. Nothing unites a nation like paying the same tax rate."

At this time, another squadsman, from a small town in western Nebraska, asked, "As you know, only yesterday a big semi-trailer truck loaded with explosives blew up in Baghdad, killing several Iraqis, mostly Shi'ites. Ironically, the killer truck bombs happened about the same time as the Iraqi Parliament announced that it had plans to move outside the US troop protected Green Zone. It's been reported that several of the Iraqi have complained that they were unprotected. There were no Iraqi police or army personnel safeguarding the area, nor was there Iraqi police or army people operating their usual check points. My question is, since the Iraqis seem to be getting worse at protecting their country as each day goes by, will the US be necessitated to again take over the operation of Iraqi security? Will that extend our stay in Iraq? These are the answers I'm seeking."

"That is the basic reason I have begun these Town Hall forums, right here in the Green Zone," Bis pointed out. "If that is to be the case, we, as the American troops that are to be assigned to re-take Baghdad, and to restore order, are entitled to know the facts. The American people are also entitled to know the true facts. We have been subjected to a series of fabrications from Bush, and from Petraeus, over the last several months, about the true status of Iraq," adding, "Does the Iraqi government have the vital interest to provide equal representation to the Iraqis? Is the Iraqi government capable of operating a government? Do the Iraqi armed forces have the ability to alone, protect Iraqis, or will they dissolve into Sunni and Shi'ite militias, go their own way, and kill their fellow Iraqis the same way they have always done?

"America must know the answers to these questions," Bis intervened. "The 7th /squadron must know the answers to these questions," adding, "This is an election year in America. All the Representatives, and one-third of the Senate, are up for election. These Congressmen must become aware of the fact that, if they continue to support an unwinnable war in the Middle East, which even the kept media can no longer hide, they will lose."

The Nebraskan chuckled, and commented, "You don't think calling our present Congress liars, or election lobbying cheats, will effect the 2008 Election, do you?"

Bis smiled, and told this story to his squadsmen, "Their once was a Senator from Oklahoma, who, in a moment of truth, said, 'You can call a Congressman a liar, a cheat, a crackpot, or a licentious old man, and it won't bother him. But if you tell him: if you continue to support an unwinnable Iraqi War, you can't win the coming election. This is a point the politician will understand.'"

"The American people, therefore, will win, and the 7th Squadron will win," Bis declared, closing out the 7th Squadron's first Town Hall Meeting, to the spontaneous applause of the squadsmen.

CHAPTER XI –
CHRISTIANITY AT
RISK

The morning following the 7th Squadron's Town Hall meeting, Bis got a knock on his semi-private room in the Squadron's barracks."Come in," Bis answered, "The door is open."

A squadsman Bis knew to be from a small town in Missouri came into the room, saying, "I'm sorry to bother you, Sergeant, but I wanted to talk to you privately before we all got busy on Squadron stuff."

Bis invited him to sit down and talk.

The Missouri squadsman continued, after accepting Bis' invitation, "You probably don't know that I am a member of the Southern Baptist Church. I am also, was, an officer in my home town church, and after this Iraqi tour in the Brigade, I intend to go to a Baptist seminary and become a preacher."

Bis did not reply, but indicated for the squadsman to go on, who then said, "I have, accordingly, on my off days, tried to help the few Christians that are still left in Baghdad and Iraq. In talking with them, I have discovered that they are subject to some strange anti-American, anti-Christian, US policies in Iraq concerning Christians," adding, "I did not want to talk about it last night, at the town hall meeting, because I did not want to be called prejudiced."

"What did you discover?" asked Bis.

"For one thing," the Missourian replied, "Iraqi Christians, particularly since the arrival of US troops, are subject to having their daughters and wives kidnapped by renegades, both Moslem Sunnis and Shi'ites, who then hold them for ransom, forcing Christian fathers to sell things to raise cash. The Muslim kidnappers also, typically, abuse the daughters, and rape the wives, while they hold them," adding, "Christians, when this happens, have no choice but to try to raise the ransom. These Iraqi Christians are understandably afraid, and several have made applications to be accepted as refugees by the US."

He continued, "Believe it or not, these Christian Iraqis have been turned down, as unacceptable, by the US State Department. It is now official US policy that if an Iraqi Christian puts together the money to pay the kidnapping Moslems the demanded ransom in order to save his wife or daughter's life, that Iraqi Christian is then also deemed by the US as a terrorist, and is forever barred from immigrating to America."

Bis' eyes widened in disbelief, as the squadsman commented, "Of course, many of these Christians, at the same time, have also been hired by the US Forces for many jobs, and this also makes Iraqi Christians traitors in the eyes of all the Iraqi Muslims, including those Sunnis and Shi'ites running the Maliki government," adding, "The Maliki people have, as such, pressured Bush and his friends, to deny Iraqi Christians the designation as refugees. They want an Iraq free of any Christian influence. Bush and Petraeus, not wanting to offend the Sunnis and Shi'ites who run the Maliki government, because they need a strategic force agreement, unbelievably, have agreed to prostrate themselves, and label these poor Christian Iraqis as terrorists."

"I can't conceive of such a thing," Bis responded.

"It breaks your heart," the Christian squadsman declared. "For instance, a Christian told me that a daughter of a friend was recently kidnapped. Her father's name was Boutros. He found some way to pay the Moslems' ten thousand dollars, and then, with his family, was forced to flee to Jordan, where he then applied to be allowed to come to America. The US officials taking his application told him, 'You have helped the terrorists, so you cannot come to America.'"

He continued, "Several Christian Iraqi fathers have also shown me horrible pictures of their children, lying dead in the Baghdad streets, with their throats slit," adding, "Other Iraqi Christians have also told me, including the threat made to the local pastor's sister, 'You are a Kaffir,' and worse, 'You work for the Americans, so you are a traitor.'

"What can be done to alert American Christian citizens about this sad state of affairs?" asked the Missourian.

"I don't know," Bis responded. "I did not know that the US government had created such a madcap way of thinking, as official US policy. I do know that the people running America, the Congress in 2004, unanimously created another stupid, anti-Christian statute."

Bis continued, "Congress, by this statute, created, and the State Department has staffed, an Office of Global Anti-Semitism. This nutty office has issued several anti-Christian statements, which in effect state and refute that what is sacredly written in the New Testament, setting forth facts, that some Jews had instigated Christ's crucifixion is classical anti-Semitism, which they label as a historic form of hate. 'State' has actually insinuated that the sacred words of the New Testament, many actually uttered by Christ himself, which historically tell of the God driven fate of Christ. It was witnessed by several thousands of then watching people relating these well-known crucifixion events. Words of hate, not Scripture, according to this State Department 'hate office', implying we don't want to embarrass or discomfort our modern day Jews. Therefore, we must change, or modify, or do whatever is necessary to erase any guilt feelings our 'can do no wrong', modern day Jewry feels. This group wants to modify or change the actual words of God and Christ, as they are written in the New Testament. Words that have defined Christians for two thousand years. Words that are revered by eighty percent of modern day American Chrisitans."

Bis continued, "That such hate legislation could have unanimously come out of our Congress is something I would never have perceived as happening in America. Most of the people in the Congress must not have known what was in this hate statute, or what was to be its effect. The practice of giving Israel everything it wants, even to the extent of changing the Christian Bible for them, has got to stop. We must inform American Christians about this law, and they have to go after each of their congressmen," adding, "This type of hate legislation is not new. The elite of several West European nations, not the people, have also allowed similar hate laws, which mandate that if a citizen, or even a pastor, merely recites the actual words of the New Testament, he will be prosecuted, and jailed, for a hate crime. In America, it is the Jewish, Anti-defamation League of B'nai B'rith that have thrown all their weight behind this congressional creation of the Office of Global Anti-Semitism. They actively seek to prosecute any person who recites, or promotes those sacred words of the New Testament, implying that Christianity is inherently anti-Semitic.

"This same State Department report, and the statements emanating from this same hate crime office, also mandates that it is equally anti-Semitic to state 'intentionally or unintentionally', that Israel persecutes Palestinians; that the Jews exert undue influence on Congress, the White House, or the media; or that American Jews are equally loyal to Israel.

"This is stupid. This is unbelievable. This is anti-Christian. This is anti-American," Bis concluded. "It will only be stopped when the American people insist on it being stopped."

"It is hard to believe, in America, a law like that could be passed," echoed the Missourian, "and passed unanimously," adding, "But in the words of America's great General William E. Odom, who died only a few weeks ago, 'Our ostrich strategy of keeping our heads buried in the sands of Iraq has done nothing but advance our enemies' interest,' and describing the invasion of Iraq as, 'the greatest strategic disaster in US history.' It is easy to see how it can happen. General Odom warned America, mostly unreported, that the US would not have gone into Iraq, 'without the strong lobbying efforts from the American-Israel PAC (AIPAC), and the neo-cons,' so it is also easy to see who is behind it."

Bis nodded in agreement, and then commented, "Anyone who has thinking cap on straight realizes that Bush was cajoled into invading Iraq by the conniving of a nest of neo-cons, with their convenient base of operations in the Department of Defense."

"They could not have done it," added the squadsman, "without the active intervention of Vice President Dick Cheney, a charter member of the neo-cons, the Israeli General Staff, and the leadership of the Likud Party in Israel."

He continued, "Getting back to my assertion that the Bush Administration is blatantly anti-Christian, and is actively forming a US policy supporting the aims of the Muslims, while at the same time punishing Christianity, is for a reason. Bush desperately wants an agreement for the US to be allowed to dominate Iraqi airspace, and have the ability to launch military operations from Iraq against Iran. At the same time,

Bush wants to be granted immunity from prosecution under Iraqi law," adding, "To get that agreement, Bush is ready and willing to sell out both American and Iraqi Christians, and to ditch two thousand years of sacred Christianity. This effort is not for America, but for the sole reason of protecting Israel."

"Not only protection," replied Bis, "but to make sure Israel remains the dominant Middle East power with the sole possession of nuclear weapons of mass destruction."

Bis continued, "General Odom was right when he associated the American Israel Public Affairs Committee, as the biggest base for those who unhesitantly, and intentionally, support Israel, including the neo-cons who engineered our stupid, tragic, invasion of Iraq. AIPAC's foundation in the Jewish-American community is gold plated. It has a membership list of one hundred thousand wealthy Jewish patrons, and is reputed to be the most influential, and most powerful lobby group in America. It is the reason Bush and the Congress fall all over themselves to provide three billion dollars a year to Israel in soft, no payback loans. AIPAC has made sure that Israel is equipped with the most modern of American military equipment, and has provided the additional three billion dollars necessary for Israel to build the twenty foot wall between Israel and the Palestinians, which has allowed Israel to settle, and now claim much of the West Bank."

Bis continued, "It has also become a rite of passage, a rite of fealty, for American presidential candidates, of both parties, to swear to the sitting conventions of

AIPAC each election year, that they are best friends to Israel. That they will insure that America will always be there to protect the interests of Israel from anyone and everyone, and that the bond between Israel and the US is perpetual and permanent. Each political party puts forth their total efforts to out promise the other," adding, "Both the Republicans and the Democrats would have us believe that you must be accepted by AIPAC, to have any chance at being elected president, or Senator, or even Representative. It has gotten out of hand. Israel should be supported, only on an objective basis, as a friendly, sovereign nation, and then only if it is also in America's best interest.

"Bush II, and both political parties, in crushing Iraqi Christians have substituted the Koran for the Bible. They have put the interests of Israel over and above the best interests of America."

The squadsman from Missouri nodded his agreement, saying, "A Christian friend wrote me, a few days ago about some missionary work he was doing in the West bank. What he told me makes me wonder if Israel really is a friend to America.

"In his letter, he told of a young German Christian Missionary who was working with Jewish Christians, Palestinian Christians, and Messianic Jews in the West Bank, and also in Israel proper. Her name was Barbara Ludwig, and she had been in Israel on behalf of an international Christian group."

He continued, "She was criminally rounded up at her hostel, at 6:00 a.m., by Israeli police, who handcuffed her, and jailed her. The police and judge told her she had violated Section 170 and 172 of the

Israeli Criminal Code, which bans 'speaking in public in a way that is offensive to people of any religion,' and, 'to pay someone to convert to another religion,' which she denied doing, and which laws are contrary to the Universal Declaration of Human Rights, which Israel has signed. It guarantees, 'everyone has the right to change his religion – to manifest his religion – or beliefs – in worship and observance,'" adding, "Miss Ludwig was told to leave Israel immediately or be jailed."

He continued, "My friend's letter pointed out that, besides the humiliation, and the anti-Christian position of the Israeli authorities, there is now pending before the Israeli Knesset, an even more stringent law which says, 'Whoever publicizes things in which there is an inducement to religious conversion, can be imprisoned for a year,'" adding, "Maybe the jailing of Christians, along with burning of the Christian New Testaments, in the West Bank, will lessen the zeal of Christians like Reverend Hagee, and his followers, to hail Israel, no matter what."

"Israel's 1948 War, where the Israeli Army drove thousands of Palestinian Christians out of Israel, and into refugee camps, and also in the Israeli-Lebanon War of 2006, which, incidentally, was supported by Bush and company, Lebanese and Jordanian Christians, in the thousands, were murdered in mass, unnecessary, saturation bombing sorties by Israeli bombers," Bis commented. "These facts also didn't lessen the Reverend Hagee's continuing praise for Israel," adding, "In 1920, Palestine was populated with twenty percent claiming they were Christians. They number only two point one percent, and lessen each day due to Israeli officially mandated persecution."

"God gave us his mercy through the life of Jesus Christ, our Savior," the Missourian noted. "It would appear that Bush, his generals, Reverend Hagee, and the Israelis have buried, or forgotten that fact," adding, "They actually seem overjoyed with bowing humbly to the Moslems."

Bis, in an effort to get to other pressing matters, strode out into the barrack proper, closing the conversation, and declared, "There is a defining German word, I am sure would be understood by Miss Ludwig. It is the word *schadenfreude.* Freely translated, it means, 'to be glad something bad happens to somebody'."

"That word fully covers the situation."

CHAPTER XII –
THE RASHAD ROAD

The relative peace and quiet of non-deployment for the 7th Squadron finally came to a screeching halt.

Two days after the arousing, and enlightening Town Hall Meeting, Bis alerted his squadsmen that the Squadron had received orders to go back into Iraqi hostilities, beginning at 4:00 a.m. the following morning. The 7th, and two other squadrons of the 711th Stryker Brigade, would proceed to Tamim Province, at all speed, to reinforce a small US garrison in the village of Rashad.

In answer to the squad's "Where is that?" chorus, Bis responded, "Tamim Province is about one hundred miles north of Baghdad. Its capital is Kirkuk, which makes it an oil rich city, and means that it is Kurdish controlled," adding, "Rashad, however, is a small village in the south part of Tamim. Its village population is mixed, with Kurds, Turkomen, and both Sunni and Shi'ite Arabs."

Bis continued, "The largest group of inhabitants, however, is the Sunni. The US garrison was situated just outside the Rashad municipal building. Since the mayor, and most of the councilmen, was Sunni, it is assumed that it was a Shi'ite group, which drove the suicide truck bomb, which, incidentally, had been passed by the garrison's challenge, because the probable Sadr Shi'ite participants had hidden their explosives under some tanned animal hides. The truck was stopped only a few feet away from the garrison, and at the front door of the municipal building, when the Shi'ites exploded it. The truck bomb killed two of the American soldiers on guard, and fifteen Iraqi municipal people, including a Sunni councilman," adding, "It is a good lesson for us all. Look at, and under, everything. Any laxness could end your life."

Bis continued, "Our three Brigade Squadrons will assemble at 3:00 a.m. tomorrow morning, at our usual departure point, and as I have told our driver, we will proceed at fifty to sixty miles per hour on the open highway between Baghdad and Rashad," adding, "We intend to make a showing of force, plus back up the garrison, for at least three days, staying in the garrison compound. From time to time, the 7th Squadron will make sweeps of the city, and of the surrounding area. Rations, and other equipment, will follow us in a truck, on the speed run."

After the announcement and the Squad had been dismissed, Tooley approached Bis asking, "Is what we're ordered to do the result of Muqtada al-Sadr's continued attacks on Iraqi government facilities?"

"I'm not sure this was Sadr's doing," Bis responded. "Rashad is a Sunni town, and the Sunni's also have an 'Awakening Council' office located in the municipal building, which could have been the target."

"The First Sergeant over at the Brigade told me that there are a few incidences, which occurred over the last few days that point to Sadr. Several gunmen trapped and then assassinated the Iraqi general who was the commanding officer in Maliki's recent offensive against Sadr's Mahdi Army in Basra," adding, "A few days later, in another Maliki ongoing crackdown against Shi'ites supporting Sadr, pushed by Petraeus and company, which was also supported by a Battalion of US soldiers, along with helicopters, and several US Air Force smart bombs, a cousin of Maliki's was killed, supposedly by bullets from those GI's involved. The cousin, Ali Abdul-Hussein was extremely close to Maliki. He is mad about it, demanding an explanation from the Americans."

"That should give Maliki another excuse to dis the Strategic Power Treaty Bush and Petraeus want," offered Bis, adding, "But then Maliki, and his associates, will never sign it anyway."

"They don't have to," agreed Tooley. "By holding out, they are still getting outrageous deals from Bush, granting most Iraqi wishes that give the Iraqi government an authorized right to murder Iraqi Christians, plus allow Maliki and his buddies to personally enrich themselves on Iraqi oil, while American taxpayers pay the total costs of the Iraqi occupation."

"It will right itself in the end," Bis said, nodding, "the American people, eventually, will take their vengeance," closing out the conversation.

The next morning's time of deployment, even at 3:00 a.m., was hot and steamy, approaching ninety degrees Fahrenheit.

"As usual," Tooley complained, putting on his sixty pounds of body armor, over his GI uniform, "It will probably reach one hundred degrees by 8:00 o'clock a.m., and one hundred twenty degrees by noon."

"And that doesn't even count the weight of the helmet, the M-4 rifle, and its ammunition, plus the ever ready, necessary water bottle," Bis commented, laughing.

"It's a good thing that a guy's body can get used to this stuff," Bis concluded, as he observed his Squad was now dressed, and ready to depart.

"Okay men, lets go," Bis ordered, leading his Squad out the barrack's door to their awaiting Stryker, which Bis had instructed their driver to retrieve from the deployment area, and to drive it to the barracks for an easy load.

"Atten-hut," Bis ordered, as they lined up in front of the Stryker.

"Remember," Bis cautioned, "there is no air conditioning, and the Stryker will be going too fast for you to ride on top," adding, "I will tell the driver to open up all the windows he can, and also the peek holes, to give you as much heat relief as possible. I do, however, want you to keep your rifle close at hand all during the speed run, just to make sure."

Bis closed out, saying, "It should take about three hours to get to Rashad."

With his Squad now fully loaded in their Stryker, and the other two participating Strykers, plus their ration's truck, safely out of the Green Zone, and now operating at fifty-five miles per hour on the open highway, Bis began to relax a little, and told Tooley to come up front.

"I want you to watch the men from time to time," Bis advised. "Let me know if you see any sign of heat, or any other problems."

After about an hour into the ride, with everyone in the Stryker showing no stress, Bis and Tooley relaxed a little more with Tooley observing, "We are getting into the area of the sovereign nation of Kurdistan. They are, in fact, a separate entity, no matter what Bush or Petraeus say about a unified Iraq."

Bis nodded, and interposed, "They have their own independent army. They also have a neck lock on the Kirkuk oil fields, which are located entirely within the Kurd's zone of operation," adding, "The Kurd Prime Minister already approved, unilaterally, several oil deals with many foreign oil companies, including some US oil companies, and they intend to honor them, and also intend to keep all the revenues from these lucrative oil deals in Kurdistan."

Tooley added, "The Brigade First Sergeant told me that Bush and Petraeus are unhappy with these Kurd oil deals, and are pressuring Maliki to try to cancel them."

"The Kurd Prime Minister told both Maliki and Petraeus that the deals are irreversible," Bis noted, "warning them they are 'dreaming' to try to set them aside."

Bis continued, "Kurdistan is a sovereign fact. They act like a part of Iraq from time to time, symbolically, but only to get more American handouts, or to prove a point in the Maliki Parliament."

"Even Saddam Hussein, symbolically, could not control the Kurds with all of his army," Tooley pointed out, adding, "Speaking of symbolism, Bush's old Press Secretary, symbolically, is now saying his Administration cooperated with the neo-cons to lie to the American people, by saying that Saddam was behind the September 11, 2001 New York Attack."

Tooley then commented, "The American public, also symbolically, was so gullible, or so uninformed, that the neo-cons and their controlled news media were able to convince sixty percent of them to actually believe it."

Bis laughed, saying, "Speaking symbolically, they successfully lied to those susceptible Americans even though the same media, for weeks before, had been telling of Saddam being reduced to the level of a pussy-cat by constant American Air Force fly overs."

"The media also failed to mention that Saddam was a bitter enemy of al-Qaeda, and had been for years," Tooley added.

Tooley continued, "The Press Secretary, however, confirmed my understanding of the facts, that Bush and his neo-cons used the power of his Administration to sell the lie that the Iraq War was necessary to preserve America from Saddam's weapons of mass destruction, when the fact was, overturning of Saddam was the neo-cons idea of democracy in Iraq, but only to protect Israel."

"This neo-con idea called 'Coercive Democracy', was actually the brainchild of those same neo-con Americans, who in 2002, were embedded in the US Defense Department, and other crucial departments of the Bush Administration," Bis agreed.

Bis continued, "They included Richard Perle, Chairman of the Defense Policy Board; Douglas Feith, Under-Secretary of Defense for Policy; and David Wurmser, Assistant to Vice-President Dick Cheney," adding, "If you wanted a preview, and the details of what actually happened, they, in 1996, authored a so-called position paper for Israel, titled, *'A Clean Break'*. This paper told Israel that they should immediately repeal the Oslo Agreements and keep Gaza and the West Bank. They suggested that to establish a coercive democracy in Iraq, to start by overthrowing Saddam Hussein and after that, America and Israel also should create a more coercive democracy by overthrowing Syria and Iran."

"A real, how-to instruction book," Tooley admitted. "Tell that to the four thousand five hundred Americans killed, and the thirty thousand maimed in Iraq. I'm sure that's not part of the neo-con position paper."

Suddenly the Stryker radio buzzed, startling Bis and Tooley. A voice, which Bis recognized as the Captain in charge of the three Strykers, came on the radio, saying, "We are about an hour out of Rashad. When we get down to fifteen minutes, each Stryker will stop, secure the area, and button up to be ready for any combat," adding, "If we are not under fire when we get to Rashad City limits, put one of your men on the heavy machine guns on top, until we make contact with the garrison."

Bis stood and announced to the Squadron, the captain's orders, and then cautioned, "Keep at the ready all the next three days, while we are in Rashad. Be particularly careful of approaching Arab women, as al-Qaeda, the Sadr Shi'ites, and the disgruntled Sunnis, are now all using women as suicide bombers, because they can hide explosives under their robes."

All things remained quiet on the Rashad front, as the three Strykers, complying with the captain's orders, entered the village and stopped. They found no resistance. In fact, the streets were almost empty of both vehicles and people.

Bis detailed the Squadron's heavy machine gun operator to the roof of the Stryker, where he kept vigil behind the menacing barrel of the weapon.

The Captain told Bis, while they were all stopped that the 7th Squadron would take the lead through the city. He then ordered the 7th, after they had made actual radio, and physical, contact with the garrison, to conduct a reconnaissance of the area, and report back to the Captain.

After passing a few streets, and intersections, the Squadron quickly came upon the Rashad courthouse section of town. It was obvious what heavy damage had been done to the surrounding area by the huge truck bomb, a few days before. It was also obvious to Bis that the location of the US garrison, and its various checkpoints leading, both to its compound, and also to the joint municipal building, with its

Americanized mayor and councilmen, along with the Sunni Awakening Council's offices, invited just such an attack from any of several Iraqi groups, protesting the American occupation.

Taking a quick look, Bis concluded, saying to Tooley, "The US troop compound should have been in an area entirely separate from the terrorist inviting municipal areas," adding, "There also should have been only one checkpoint, and that should have been at least a block away from the municipal entrance. US guards should have been protecting the checkpoint, with GI's posted on the side streets."

The radio again broke up their conversation, but this time it was an officer, describing himself as the US Army Major, commanding the compound, breaking into the 7th Squadron's radio, welcoming the Strykers. The Major began by bragging about the invulnerability of his inviting, complicated, defense system, which proved to be very vulnerable.

Bis introduced himself, and told the Major that his Stryker Squadron had been designated as the first contact unit.

The Major continued to brag about his military installation, saying, "We don't need to be relieved, or to be given assistance. We have a good understanding with the local municipal officer," adding, "Come on in, and we will feed you breakfast."

Bis acknowledged the radio conversation with the Major, saying, "We will join you with a three man squad shortly," adding, "Thanks, but we have made our own arrangements to eat," and turned off the radio.

"The Major still does not realize his mistakes," Tooley acknowledged.

"To quote George Eliot, a well known writer, 'Blessed is the man who, having nothing to say, abstains from giving wordy evidence of the fact,'" Bis commented, adding, "It will be difficult for a sergeant to tell a major he is a fool."

Chapter XIII – Rashad Rhapsody

It was still only eight o'clock a.m. on that Rashad morning of June 19, 2008. It had been five hours since his 7th Squadron left their barracks in the Green Zone, but it seemed like five days. The heat was already boiling at one hundred fifteen degrees Fahrenheit, as Bis, and two of his Squad, made their way from their Stryker to the "Friendly" compound major.

Bis saluted the Major as they met, and asked, "Has there been any additional attacks on you, or the municipal building, since the truck bomb?"

The Major returned the salute, and answered in the negative.

Bis noted that there were only two of the Major's men guarding the compound perimeter, and asked where the rest were.

"Sergeant, I will answer that question only to an officer of a rank higher than mine," the Major commented, in a shout-like voice. "I don't intend to be monitored by a sergeant."

"Yes, Sir," Bis continued. "My Captain asked me to check these things, and report back to him. I'll have him report to you, Sir," adding, "The Captain did want me to inform you that his orders direct that our Strykers conduct a show of force in Rashad, and in the surrounding area as soon as we get here," adding, "We are also ordered to inspect, and improve, your compound defenses."

The Major turned bright red, as he sputtered something unintelligible, turned on his heels, and went back into his municipal building-compound combination office.

Bis immediately radioed his Captain and gave him a full report.

The Captain made no reply, for a minute, and then said only, "Return to your Stryker. You will be designated as the lead Stryker in our show of force. We start from the compound, which is in the center of Rashad. The map shows only ninety degree intersections, so we can work our way on the streets north to the city limits, then go five miles north, or so, to a connecting road, which goes west for about two miles. Then back south for ten miles, then east for two miles, to the south Rashad city limits. Then we go intersection by intersection in south Rashad back to the municipal building," adding, "That should be a sufficient show of force."

The show of force went well. Everything went without a hitch, and the smooth operating three Strykers, moving in tandem, did display an exhilarating show of force, impressing the inhabitants of Rashad. They were all back in the compound by eleven o'clock a.m. The Captain took the lead, and told Bis, by radio, to follow him into the compound perimeter. "Find a good location for the three Stryker Squadrons to habituate for the next three days," the Captain ordered. He closed by saying he would leave his Stryker at that time and go visit with the Major.

Bis moved through the gate and pulled his Stryker into a fairly clear area in the center of the compound. He then stopped and radioed to the sergeants commanding the other combat vehicles. Bis told them to park alongside. He also invited the sergeants, after they had posted one of their men to man the M-240 machine guns on top of their Strykers, to join Bis in walking the entire perimeter of the compound.

As Bis and one of the two sergeants proceeded with their long, hot, perimeter inspection, Bis again noted that there were still only two perimeter guards. There were also only two guards posted at the front gate, whose job it was to check and to clear anyone coming into the municipal compound combination.

It was two US gate guards that were killed in the truck explosion.

Bis also noted, the compound was completely surrounded by city streets, with one and two story buildings clustered on most of the narrow streets, all within a half block or less of the compound's perimeter. The compound itself had been placed on the original municipal building's graveled parking area.

"It probably made sense from being an open area, and from a convenience point of view," Bis thought, *"But not from a security viewpoint."*

When they returned back to their Strykers, the Captain had finished his meeting with the Major, and had told the gunners to stand down. He did not go into what they said to each other, but the Captain told Bis, "We have our orders, and we will carry them out," obviously he was not too happy with his exposure to the Major.

Bis saluted and reported, "Sir, the compound is in the most vulnerable place in Rashad. It is undefendable, and only invites attacks by any Iraqi who is against the US insistence and interference with Muslims in the running of their local governments."

"Draw up a plan showing where in Rashad the compound should be placed," the Captain commented, "Along with any suggested defenses," adding, "I'll look it over and also take it to the Major later."

"Sir," continued Bis, "I don't think Sadr's boys are through with Rashad yet. The Sunnis control the town. The Mayor and City Council are part and parcel with the old Hussein Awakening Council," adding, "I think sometime in the next few days, this town, and all the GI's in it, are going to be in one big firefight."

After thinking about it for a minute, the Captain interposed, "What do you have in mind?"

"Get on the radio, and have Brigade send us out a Joint Terminal Air Controller, to serve as a spotter here on the ground in Rashad. The spotter can direct planes from the 14th Fighter Squadron, with their laser guided five hundred pound bombs they can blast any enemy house or shop firing on us, with a real exact precision you can't get from any other fire source," adding, "They fly over Baghdad most days, so it would not inconvenience them."

Bis continued, "Also, Sir, as bad as the protection is, since we are going to be here three days, and the compound perimeter is already permanently set, it would take a full battalion to move the compound now. I would suggest, until we get additional boots on the ground, and the agreement of the Major to move it, that we add part of one of our squads to the perimeter defense, including the front gate. I would also suggest, for now, we park our Strykers in the fairly open area I've discovered in the northwestern part of the compound. We should then cut the perimeter wire at that point to allow us to come and go at will, on our shows of force," adding, "We should also set up our own gate, along with our own guards. Beginning in the morning, we should assign three men from one squadron, to alternate, and to walk the side streets adjacent to our new entrance."

"Finally," Bis declared, "We should sleep outside in our bags, next to our Strykers, and live on 'C' rations for the next two and one-half days," adding, "It might be inconvenient, an attack may never come, but the situation is ripe for it, and I feel it is the prudent thing to do."

The Captain listened carefully to this sergeant he had learned to respect over the last several weeks they had been deployed together in Iraq. Bis had properly diagnosed the solutions to most of their combat assignments, and had earned the Captain's trust.

The officer, accordingly, told Bis, "Set up your approved spot for our Strykers for the next three days. Get everything in order, and assigned, as far as posting guards for the next twenty-four hours. Get everything in readiness to construct the new gate," adding, "I will go and discuss all these things with the Major," smiling, "but not until after I request Battalion to send us a Joint Terminal Air Controller, to be here in the morning."

Bis smiled broadly, and gave the Captain a smart salute.

It was 3:00 a.m. the following morning as Tooley gently woke Bis, saying, "The guards at our gate, the same having been unwired, reconstructed, and manned the night before, along with our guards walking the side streets, have reported a lot of unusual activity in those areas next to the compound's front gate."

"What kind of activity?" questioned Bis, wiping sleep out of his eyes.

"They see a lot of lights going on and off in those close in buildings. Many people seem to be, for no reason, walking those streets, and then disappearing into the buildings," Tooley responded.

Bis zipped himself out of his sleeping bag, and while pulling on his boots, told Tooley, "Alert our Squadron. Have them report, as soon as possible, to me, fully dressed with armor, and with their M-4's and plenty of ammunition," adding, "Also tell our Stryker driver to report."

While Tooley was performing those duties, Bis finished putting on his uniform and armor, and checked his M-4 carbine. He then contacted his Captain by radio, and told him what was transpiring.

The Captain responded, saying, "I will notify the other two Strykers, and order their Squadrons to report to you."

At 3:30 a.m., all three Squadrons were dressed, armed, and armored, and standing around Bis' Stryker, as the Captain strode up and, for emphasis, put his arm around Bis' shoulder, saying, "Sergeant, you were obviously absolutely correct about the eminence of an enemy terrorist attack. Where will it begin?"

Bis responded, "All the unusual activity seems to be located around the close in buildings on both sides of the Major's front gate," adding, "Our guards have not reported any enemy vehicles, so they probably don't have heavy weapons, but we can probably expect mortars, rockets, and grenades, along with heavy rifle fire."

Just then, a guard from the Squadron's new gate ran up and told the Captain, "A Humvee and two trucks are at the gate. They say they were sent by Battalion to direct air strikes, and were told to enter by our gate, and to report directly to the Captain."

The Captain let out a cheer, and told the guard to direct the Ground Controller and his crew to him.

"That is a big break," Bis told the Captain. "I have a hunch we will need them once the firefight gets heavy, and we can pinpoint the location of the terrorist's command post, and also where their heavy fire is coming from."

Bis continued, "All three of our Strykers, with men manning the M-240 machine guns, should be pulled close to the main gate. Their drivers must be ready to pull them up to respond to the terrorists, once they start their attack," adding, "Each of our Squadrons should be fully armed and ready, using their Strykers as a mobile fort, first, to direct mass fire where the Captain determines it would best be utilized, and, second, to occupy, and control the areas where the Captain decides the fighter planes should lob in their precision laser guided, five hundred pound bombs. Only, however, after they have done their work," he cautioned.

The Captain then took over his Squadrons, issuing orders in compliance with Bis' carefully thought out defense plan.

The crews of all three Strykers hastened to complete their part in defending their positions.

The Ground Controller, from Joint Terminal Air, was thoroughly briefed on the defense situation, and he proceeded to set up his crew in the best position to call in air strikes when needed.

As all this activity was going on, the Captain, Tooley, and Bis, gathered together, where they could best direct the continuing defenses.

Tooley commented, "After this fight, we better find another better location for the compound."

Bis stood, forced a laugh, frowned, and then responded, "When the planes from the 14th Fighter Squadron, if they operate as they usually do, finalize their strikes on those close in buildings surrounding the front gate, there will no longer be a defense problem with the compound. The problems I see now will no longer be a problem."

"What do you mean?" asked the Captain.

"I mean there will be no defense problem, because there will be no buildings."

Chapter XIV – Rashad – Ravaged and Rescued

The eastern sky in Iraq, at 4:30 a.m., was beginning to turn from black-black to blackish-whitish. It was not quite dawn. On this June 21st day, some larger features of the city, surrounding the compound, were becoming more visible.

Bis had earlier calculated the odds. The three Stryker Squadrons, plus their auxiliaries added up to fifty-five GI's of various ranks and specialties. The Major's troop number was set at about a company size, or maybe sixty-five GI's of various competencies.

"One hundred twenty US troops pitted against, who knows how many, Islamic terrorists," Bis thought to himself, *"The odds are not good, but better than they were."*

The Air Force Sergeant, who had arrived in Rashad as the Ground Controller for the Fighter Squadron's Joint Terminal Air, interrupted Bis and the Captain, as he reported to Bis' Captain, saying, "My men are all set, and I have been in personal radio contact with two of the jet fighters from the 14th Squadron. They have just taken off from their auxiliary base near Baghdad, and will be cruising in an area about fifty miles from Rashad," adding, "If you have a mission for them, I can get them here in five minutes."

The Captain returned his salute, thanking him, and as the Air Force Sergeant was leaving, Bis asked, "Are you and your men armed?"

The Air Force Sergeant responded, "We have a couple of .45's in the Humvee."

Bis looked at the Captain, and by eye contact, both agreed to a solution, as the Captain told the Air Force Sergeant, "You and your men report to the supply truck parked next to the Strykers. I'll tell them to issue an M-4 Carbine each to you and your men, with sufficient ammo to keep you armed for a sufficient period."

The Sergeant appeared not to understand, and Bis told him, "We expect you to man your ground control facilities first, but we are also likely to be involved with an overwhelming enemy, Muslim assault, by small arms fire, indirect fire, and rocket propelled grenades. They are likely to come at us from all directions. The Captain wants to make sure you are able to defend yourself in the area he has assigned you."

The Air Force Sergeant smiled at Bis, and them commented, "I understand. Me and my guys didn't figure we would have to become Army riflemen, but I've got a good, versatile crew, and if we have to, we can do as well as the Army."

Bis smiled as the Sergeant left them, thinking, "*They will be alright.*"

Tooley broke into Bis' thoughts as the noise of the Stryker combat vehicles starting up filled the compound, saying, "The Strykers are moving into position. I'll make sure they move to a place, not too far, but also not too close to the front gate." Bis nodded an okay as Tooley left.

Bis and the Captain, as the Strykers moved by, followed them close behind, setting up their command post in about the center of their final waiting positions. Bis then declaring with a satisfaction, "The Strykers are in position. The Squadrons are armed and set. The ground controller is ready, and we are ready."

Bis mentioned to the Captain that there were still only two of the Major's men guarding the front gate. The Captain interposed, "I told him to get his men ready for an attack, but he said he had been assured by the Sunni Mayor that the compound was not in any danger of attack," adding, "He then noted that he was a Major, and I was a Captain, and he would command his men."

Bis shook his head sadly. Suddenly he became aware of the quickly growing daylight. Looking at his watch he declared, "Its five a.m., and it is light enough now for the terrorists to function. If they are going to attack, they will show in the next half hour."

No sooner had these words left his mouth, than Bis noticed a US Army dump truck approaching the front gate. It was at that time, a block away. As it got within a half block, Bis could see the lone occupant was wearing a US Army uniform.

Bis knew, instinctively, that this was a suicide truck, trying to appear as American. Realizing he had no time to explain, he quickly moved over to his 7th Squadron riflemen, who were already poised with their rifles at the ready, and ordered them, plus the Squadman manning the Stryker's machine gun, to commence firing immediately at the dump truck.'

The rifle racket startled everyone in the compound. Bis, notwithstanding, ordered the firing to continue, as the oncoming truck did not appear to be affected. The dump truck was approaching within three hundred yards of the compound's front gate, when suddenly, the rifle bullets took hold, causing the truck, to veer off to the side, into one of the buildings, and then, with unexpected violence, it blew up. The explosion was so enormous that the building it hit almost completely disappeared, sending debris in every direction, even reaching the Stryker's area, peppering them with small pellets.

The blast also left a big hole in the street, with only a few recognizable parts of the dump truck scattered in the area. The blast's concussion was so great that it, involuntarily, pushed and rolled the Major's two guards several feet from their posts, and severed the wooden cross bar that was used to stop vehicles and people.

The Captain, followed by Tooley, ran up to Bis, congratulating him on his premonition, as Bis, at the same time, lauded his squadmen for following his orders without question.

"In another thirty seconds, that truck would have creamed the front gate, and destroyed the municipal building," the Captain admitted.

Dozens of our men, and the Major's men, would have been killed, or seriously hurt," Tooley interposed, adding, "Bis, you are a hero."

The back slapping came to an end, however, as the machine gunner on top of Bis' Stryker yelled, "Look out. People are emerging everywhere from either side of the blown up building. Could be a couple hundred of them. All men and carrying AK-47's and rocket pads."

The Stryker crews located on the opposite side of the 7th, also screamed, "Get ready. There are so many of them, they look like ants coming out of an anthill."

Several volleys of terrorist rifle fire suddenly erupted, creating the ding, ding, ding, of the spent bullets striking all over the compound. Some of the bullets, however, were not spent, as cries could be heard, yelling, "Medic", from the area of the municipal building, where the Major's barracks were located.

Bis and the Captain mutually agreed, it was now time to move their three Strykers forward, guns blazing, to the area of the front gate. Their M-240 machine guns, plus the consolidated, concentrated, M-4 rifle fire threw an enormous amount of fire power, raking the enemy buildings, effectively on both sides of the narrow streets.

Several militants emerged, and were watched fearfully by Bis, Tooley, and the Captain. They, being in such great numbers, were able to move through the heavy fire into the municipal building, which also housed the Major's men.

Gunfire suddenly and viciously erupted in the compound building, as the Major's men sounded like they were attempting to defend themselves. The fire fight sounded heavy and ominous.

Tooley, who had been told to closely watch the remaining buildings not affected by the exploded dump truck on the narrow Rashad streets, informed Bis and the Captain, "I think I have pinpointed the buildings where the Muslims have concentrated their mortars, and rocket launchers, and also the building where those terrorists, who appear to be the obvious leaders seem to be reporting."

Bis looked, as Tooley pointed them out, and then, agreeing, directed the suspected buildings information to the attention of the Captain.

As the Captain, Bis and Tooley all confirmed that they could identify the terrorists' strongholds, the Captain told Tooley to run and bring the Air Force Sergeant to him, telling Bis, as Tooley left, "These are ideal targets for the jet fighters' laser bombs," adding, "The big problem is they are only three hundred to five hundred yards from the front gate, and the Major's municipal-compound building."

Bis, realizing the problem, nodded in agreement, and commented, "It could be lethal to some of our troops if the bombs are only a little bit off."

Tooley returned shortly with the Air Force Sergeant, who had with him two of his men, one lugging on his back the radio equipment used to contact and direct the pilots, and the other carrying a map case.

The Sergeant saluted, after which the Captain told him, "We think we have the terrorists' stronghold centers located, but they are so close, we don't know if we can use your pilots."

"Point them out to me, Sir," the Air Force Sergeant responded, as he thumbed through his map case, and finding the appropriate one, laid it in front of the captain, Bis, and Tooley.

Tooley was the first to react, using his finger to mark what he considered the two command center enemy buildings. Bis looked, and agreed. The Captain nodded.

"They are close in," interposed the Sergeant, "The one building is only three hundred yards or so from the gate."

As if to give visual effect to their findings, suddenly flashes from the close in building, revealed several rockets being released, each rocket carrying deadly grenades. They seemed to fill the sky, and came from every possible nook and cranny of the suspect building.

Bis, realizing the rocket danger, yelled, "Take cover. Drop," as orange-yellow explosions hit various parts of the compound.

"We will have to take a chance on your fighters," Bis declared, addressing the Sergeant, "Radio the information to them as quickly as possible."

While the ground controllers were working out the details on the precision bomb strike, Bis told the Captain, as both nervously watched several more of the enemy move out of the suspect buildings and toward the ongoing battle at the municipal building, saying, "It would be wise to move our Stryker Squadrons back, at least five hundred yards, when we know the fighter planes are coming in with their five hundred pound laser bombs," adding, "After the bombs do their work, and I am praying they work as they are supposed to, those problem areas should no longer be a problem," adding, "We should then move two of our Strykers and their squadrons to the front of the municipal building and use the probable devastating effect, on the bomb confused terrorists, to charge the municipal building, clean it out of enemy gunners, and rescue what's left of the Major's men."

The Captain nodded in assent, as the ground controller told both, "We are ready. Our maps, and the maps and flyovers of our pilots agree," adding, "We should be able to take out both suspect enemy buildings, and still be within two hundred yards of any friendlies."

The Captain, with such information, ordered the controller to proceed with his mission, as the Sergeant, at the same time, admitted, "I can't, however, vouch for the safety of anyone else in any buildings abutting the targeted ones."

Bis saluted the Captain, telling him he was leaving the command post to set up the attack on the municipal building following the hoped for results of the precision bombing.

After pulling the troops back from the front gate, Bis gathered all the personnel from all three Strykers together, and instructed both the 7th and another, to be prepared to move their two Squads, plus the combat vehicles to the front of the municipal building, as soon as the bombing was over. The other Stryker was instructed to move back up to guard the destroyed front gate area.

The few minutes it took to so direct the squadmen, was all the time it took before the droning, distinct sounds of two jet fighters could be heard, and then seen, as suddenly, without further warning, they swooped low, diving toward Rashad's suspected enemy buildings.

Bis ordered everyone to take immediate cover. Bis, himself, dove to the ground beside the 7th combat vehicle, and as he did, he was clearly moved, and lifted to one side by the huge concussions created by the two five hundred pound laser bombs, striking, what Bis prayed was only the suspect buildings.

As Bis struggled to get to his feet after the bombs hit, he looked toward the narrow Rashad streets to try to judge the effect of the lasers, and also to try to make sure that none of the US troops had been hit.

Bis could not believe his eyes, as Tooley, in the meantime, had moved to his right side, telling the Corporal, "My God. The buildings are completely gone. There is nothing left on either side but blank space."

"I don't see any real, permanent damage to the compound," Tooley commented, "But the municipal building looks like it sustained some damage."

Descending upon them was an eerie quiet, both in the compound, and also out in the terrorist held remaining buildings, and narrow streets, as Bis moved through his strewn out squadron troopers, urging them to get up, and to get their rifles ready.

When they looked ready and alert, Bis then ordered the driver of the Squadron's Stryker vehicle, to move it forward toward the front of the municipal building, following which he yelled to his men, "Follow me."

The mere five minutes it took to set up and move his men the few hundred yards forward with the Stryker in front of them as a moving fort, seemed like years. They easily, and without resistance, reached the municipal building without incident. The attacking Moslem enemy seemed brain deadened and negligent by the bombs.

But that quickly changed, as Bis, followed by his Squad, entered the blown off huge front doors, encountering, all at once, two terrorists, who were surprised by Bis, and his Squad. They tried to bring their shouldered AK-47's to bear, but were immediately taken out by Bis and his troopers.

The fierce firefight continued for a few additional minutes, inside the building, as Bis, Tooley and the two Squadrons faced thirty to forty enemy terrorists, in a do or die battle, but Bis' GI's had the advantage of surprise and fire power, and it was soon over.

Bis, in the quiet victory after battle, moved to the center of the building, searching in vain, for the Major, and his troops.

The inside was a mess. Doors were off. Panels and other parts of the structure had been stripped from the walls and used as defenses, and were strewn everywhere. Bis pulled three terrorist bodies laying dead on the floor to one side, as they blocked the front of the closed off, enormous big room, which he knew was used by the Major as his office, and as his command center. He also was drawn to the room by muffled cries of "Medic. For God's sake, get me a Medic."

Bis moved hastily to the office door, intending to enter and help. As he did so, Tooley joined him, warning, "Be careful you don't get shot by super scared GI's. Sit down and plan this move," he cautioned.

Tooley also told Bis that he had thoroughly inspected the lower floor, where many of the terrorists had met their fatal fate. He also had three men of the Squadron searching the second floor, adding, "This little war is over, and the big hero of the northern front is Otto Bismarck."

Bis nodded, then suggested as the medic moan began again, "You push the door open, and both of us will duck to see if anyone shoots at us."

Tooley, with great caution, pushed, and as the big paneled door swung slowly open, it was immediately peppered with bullets, the door shot into by remnants of the Major's men, hidden behind overturned desks and chairs.

"This is Sergeant Bis of the 7th Stryker Squadron," Bis called out. "We have cleaned out the Moslem terrorists in the building, and you are safe."

The gunfire abruptly stopped, and a voice called out, "Sergeant, I know who you are. Show yourself, and then I will believe you."

With this challenge, Bis prepared to show himself, even in the face of the possible danger, which Tooley again warned of, contending the risk was too high, "Let me get some troops and a loud speaker."

Bis laughed, pooh-poohing the situation, saying, "These are American GI's. Like T.S. Elliot said, as Bis dug a quote from his American Literature background, 'Only those who will risk going too far, can possibly find out how far one can go.'"

"This is no time for a lecture," Tooley responded, "But go ahead. I will cover you."

Bis, holding both arms high as he slowly appeared in the doorway, saying, "I hope you guys made it."

"It is you, Sergeant," agreed the questioning rifleman in the Major's office, who then stood and cheered.

Bis and Tooley cautiously entered the big room, moving obstructions to one side.

They sadly viewed at least ten GI's dead, in various gruesome stances in the forepart of the room.

"We also have twelve wounded," the rifleman volunteered, as Bis and Tooley made their way toward him.

Clearing away the last overturned desk, Bis suddenly came onto the dead body of the Major, displaying a bullet hole right in the center of his forehead.

"At least he died facing the enemy," Tooley observed, adding, "I would not be surprised if he was actually shot by his friend, the Sunni Mayor of Rashad, who assured the Major there was no danger of a terrorist attack."

"I've got twenty scared men with me back here," the US rifleman interposed. "Most are file clerks, but they did a good job defending. The rest of our crew is up on the second floor. I don't know their fate."

Bis, satisfied that all the Major's men, and all the terrorists in the building had been accounted for, sat down, exhausted, mentally and physically.

After a few minutes, however, necessity required he radio contact his Captain, and Bis told him the building was under Stryker control and, by the grace of God, there were no Stryker casualties.

The Captain responded, "The laser bombs were the key. Nothing survived in those buildings. The terrorists were completely evaporated," contending it was a suitable dispatch of those kill crazy, Muslim worms, then asking, "How is the Major?"

Listening to Bis' conversation, Tooley thought to himself, and of a quote of his own from a bit of literature, he remembered from his high school days, the jest of it being, *"If someone or some group makes themselves a worm, he, or they, can't complain if they are trampled on,"* Tooley, did not distinguish the identity of the worm.

Chapter XV –
Happy Fourth Of July

A week and a half had gone by since Bis brought his three Strykers, basking in victory, back to the Green Zone.

Baghdad is never a very pleasant place to be in summer or winter, war or peace, win or lose, but it is made much sweeter in victory.

Talk of the three squadrons, their winning Rashad escapade, and their fighting spirit, was on everyone's lips. Each individual squadman was feted and treated like a hero. The Captain and Bis, both, had been nominated for a Silver Star.

It was truly embarrassing to Bis who considered their Rashad win as only a display of normal military competence, which should be in the inventory of every commander of men.

He told Tooley to squelch talk of this Silver Star stuff as being unnecessary, but his Corporal, laughing, responded, "They have so few genuine heroes that no one is going to stop this one," adding, "Besides, if anyone in the Rashad fight is a hero, its you."

Tooley continued, "You are a real hero in my eyes, not only for the win, but also because not a single Stryker was lost."

Tooley and Bis, finishing their hero discussion, wandered out of their Green Zone barracks, with Bis asking, "Where do you want to go for dinner?" adding,, "Since this is July 4, 2008, America's birthday. I would like to honor the city of Macon, Georgia, home of Corporal Patrick Tooley, and also the home of an ongoing love, and preservation of American heritage, by America's southern contingent, dating from the signing of the Declaration, to the twenty-first century."

Bis laughed, and giving Tooley an appreciative slap on the back, mirthfully suggested, "How about dining at 'Toot Snores'," chuckling at the mislabeling, "or at 'Top of the Fart', I mean Mart," he corrected.

"How about dining at the exclusive, reclusive, NCO Mess Hall," Tooley replied, laughing, "The only Baghdad dining facility, featuring such exquisite cuisine as hash, ham and eggs, and meat balls," adding, "nestled in the beautiful Tigris River Valley, and entered by invitation only, it is truly the eater's paradise."

"It is done," Bis replied, giving Tooley another pat on the back, "That is, if we can get in without a reservation."

Seated at one of the few lone tables in the NCO Mess, Tooley exclaimed, "Well at least my ham and eggs is a good southern treat, no matter what the occasion."

"Can't be beat," Bis responded, "But I can understand the mess sergeant's reluctance not to serve Pheasant-Under-Glass. The United States is broke. We can't afford anything better."

"The only superpower in the world, broke," Tooley interjected. "I don't believe it," raising his hands in mock horror.

"The US Senate has just voted to spend one hundred sixty-five billion dollars to fund the Iraq and Afghanistan wars," Bis pointed out, "But America is so deep in debt that each and every funding dollar will have to be borrowed from such places as China, Russia, or Europe. When Bush became our beloved president, oil was twenty-five dollars a barrel, now its one hundred forty dollars a barrel. The dollar has depreciated sixty percent against the Euro in just that short time span," adding, "The US is not only broke, we are super broke."

Tooley, taking a bite of his Georgia ham, nodded in agreement, and commented, "But American incomes are not rising to keep pace with the additional costs, that is except for the coddled elite, rich," adding, "What is so disheartening is that the political people who run our country, both Republicans and Democrats, as they also observe America falling down the world ladder, just as we do, **DO NOT CARE!**"

Bis looked hesitantly around the NCO Mess, then, animating with his right arm, said, "The latest news admits that the US Army desperately needs troops in Afghanistan," adding, "The Chair of the Joint Chiefs now confirms that the only available troops would have to be taken out of Iraq."

"The Brigade First Sergeant confided to me," Tooley then admitted, "One of our Green Zone Strykers could get the call. What do you think of that?"

"It depends," Bis responded. "I certainly have no love for Iraq," adding, "Prime Minister Nouri al-Maliki is also pushing hard for a US troop withdrawal at the same time, and is quoted as saying, 'The goal is to end the presence of foreign troops.'"

"He obviously has no love for the American GI, along with his buddies, al-Sadr, al-Sustani, the Sunnis, the Shi'ites, and al-Qaeda," Tooley laughed.

"In fact," Bis commented, "Bush, Petraeus, and their neo-con handlers, may not have any choice."

"What do you mean," asked Tooley.

"I mean Hoshyar Zebari, a Kurd who is Iraq's Foreign Minister," Bis replied. "He just returned from Washington, and after talking with Bush and the Pentagon, told the Iraqi Parliament that Bush has made major concessions on what he will accept in his strategic security agreement," adding, "Zebari contends Bush has now made major concessions to Maliki on two crucial demands, one is the immunity from prosecution by Iraqi Law of all Americans operating in Iraq, and two, Bush is now willing to relinquish control of much of Iraqi airspace."

"Maybe it would be a wise move to get out of Iraq, if we all can be put in jail by Iraqi judges," Tooley declared. "They don't have much in the way of rights here," he chuckled.

"But to go to Afghanistan might be jumping out of the frying pan, and into the burner," Bis countered, adding, "It might be more wise to give the Afghan idea a little more time. Maybe the Pentagon would agree to a Mid East shortened tour, and I could get my Squadron home early."

"Don't hold your breath," Tooley laughed, "but you are right. We should give any Afghan deal time to ripen with concession. If Maliki can do it, the 711th Stryker Brigade should too."

We also should be concerned about the fate of American GI's remaining in Iraq," Bis responded. "I think Maliki is being overly optimistic about his government troops being able to control Iraq, when US troops are reduced to a power losing critical level. When we reach that point, Sadr could re-awaken his Mahdi Army to try to take over Iraq for his Shi'ites. At the same time, the former Hussein Sunnis, now re-armed by Bush and our generals, could reopen their sleeping Sunni armies to try to blunt any Sadr Shi'ite takeover, and to protect their pre-Saddam, Sunni territory."

"Don't forget that the Kurds would also use the opportunity to solemnly declare a sovereign Kurdistan," Tooley commented, adding, "It would be the same centuries old thing over again, Shi'ites killing Sunnis, Sunnis killing Shi'ites, and both attacking Kurds."

"Except this time," Bis contended, "America is broke. Its military is scattered, and its equipment rendered mostly unusable," adding, "US Forces could easily get caught between warring Sunnis and Shi'ites, both who have no love for Americans, and make it extremely difficult for our troops to depart Iraq, even if it is desires by all the parties."

Tooley then interposed, "There is no question, Iraq will quickly break up into the same three separate entities. The whole Middle East will be back to square one, once American troops are gone, or don't have the numbers to stop them."

"Our misadventure recently in Rashad," Bis pointed out, "is just part of this continuing hate and distrust of the Sunni and the Shi'ite. The Rashad attackers were Shi'ites. They were trying to destroy a reinstituted Saddam Hussein Sunni mayor and city council, who had earlier forced a takeover of the previous Sadr Shi'ite mayor and city council. The Sunni takeover, ironically, was instigated, and bankrolled, by Bush and his pals, in support of their surge," adding, "It is the main reason the terrorists in Rashad were delighted to attack our troops."

"You can also see the Sadr verses Sunni fight manifesting itself in Maliki's recent decision to delay the October 1st Iraqi Provincial Elections," Tooley contended. "The Sunnis, as a result, are literally up in arms."

"The October elections are strongly backed by Bush and Petraeus," Bis added, "It would be a big setback for the neo-cons' plans if those elections don't go as planned."

Bis continued, "These provincial elections were favorably viewed by the Sunnis, as a sure US backed way of developing more representatives, and thereby, more influence in the Maliki Parliament, especially in those provinces where the Sunni tribes are still a majority," adding, "If the elections are now moved forward in perpetuity, the Sunnis will likely take up their armed conflict again with renewed vigor. Any Bush momentum to politically stabilize the Maliki government is likely to falter," adding, "I think the Maliki government will involuntarily dissolve regardless of whether we pull out of Iraq or not. The Bush-Petraeus move to bring more Sunnis into the government, as you said, will only reignite the longstanding conflict between Sunni and Shi'ite. It is in the very nature of the Emirs, who run Islam, for Sunnis to hate Shi'ites, Shiites to hate Sunnis, and both to hate Christianity. It seems to be inbred in both sects."

"Delaying the elections would also rile the Kurds, who violently oppose a proposed Maliki referendum to divide equally the Kirkuk Province seats," Tooley interposed. "The Kurds claim the city of Kirkuk as their own, and will not take less then all the representatives from that area," adding, "Any change, and the Kurds will pull out of the Maliki government."

Bis, nodding in agreement, said, "Not only that, but the election delay also puts into doubt a Maliki-Bush, must have, legislation pending in the Iraqi Parliament, which allocates any oil funds, raised in the oil rich Kirkuk area, to all three Iraqi sect areas," adding, "The Kurds will never agree to that, and, as we have seen in the past, the Kurds intend at all costs, to keep every bit of those oil proceeds. They also want a Kirkuk referendum on permitting the people of that city to vote on allowing them to be part of the Kurd area only."

Bis continued, "Any talk of the 711th Stryker Brigade suddenly being transferred to Afghanistan is extremely premature," adding, "It is highly improbable that any sane president, any sane Pentagon, or any sane Congress, in the face of continued renewed Shi'ite-Sunni violence, continued failure of the so-called Maliki Iraqi Army assuming effective military control of Iraq with any degree of certainty, and the continued provincial election equivocation, would, under those circumstances, pull a Brigade out of Iraq in order to send it to Afghanistan."

"Are you kidding," Tooley responded. "We are talking about an American president, and an American vice-president, many in Congress, and the entire Israeli leadership, who are brainlessly still pushing hard for an excuse to bomb Iran, even in the face of all the Iraqi problems you have cited."

"They wouldn't dare it," Bis answered. "If they did, it would be an example of the classic 'Death Wish'. The entire Middle East would be inflamed. Everything would fall apart," adding, "The American troops, both in Iraq and Afghanistan, would be at extreme risk. The American people, at least those that understand, would not stand for such an unthinking escalation. Even those brain dead Americans, who usually support what the TV tells them to, would storm the Congress with pitchforks."

"Don't be too sure of that," Tooley related. "Stranger things have happened."

Bis laughed, and then standing, picking up his coffee cup, and raising it to a proper toasting height, declared, "Happy Birthday America. You have got lots of problems, but you always have lots of problems. You have a bunch of traitorous incompetents running your Executive Branch, along with those running the military establishment. But eight times out of ten, the American people elect, and present you with similar incompetents. You have a Congress that, for the most part, is more interested in lining their own pockets with lobbyist cash, than in protecting America. But again the American electorate has consistently provided you with a Congress made up of a dearth of statesmen, but an abundance of conceited, power hungry, illiterate tools of various Tammany Halls."

Tooley smiled, stood and brought the rim of his coffee cup against Bis' cup, echoing, "A very Happy Birthday America," adding, "It isn't often that I get invited to such a prestigious birthday party. I am at an unaccustomed loss of words," laughing, "However, I am sure I will find some."

Tooley continued, "America, somehow always finds its way back to sanity and to its Constitution. What has happened in Iraq will, in time, be only a bad memory, and American school children will be taught, with their history books declaring, 'A funny thing happened to America on the way to and from Iraq.'"

The remark caused Bis to laugh so hard he had to put his coffee up down on the table. He confided, between giggles, to Tooley, "The only quote I can think of, comparable to your, some how found remarks, is one attributed to Lyn Nofziger, the magnificent, incomparable aide to Ronald Reagan, who said, straight faced, 'I sometimes lie awake at night trying to think of something funny that Richard Nixon said.'"

Chapter XVI -
Islam

Tuesday, July 15, 2008, proved to be the same hot, boring day as July 14th was.

While Bis was happy his 7th Stryker Squadron was kept in official "Rest and Recreation" at their barracks in the Green Zone, the lack of deployment did not help to pass the time.

To keep his squadron from growing stale, or developing negligent habits, Bis and Tooley had devised an every other day visit to the, all-around gymnasium available to the troops located in the Zone, but actually used by only a few of them. Bis would take half the Squad one day, and Tooley would take the other half, the next day.

This day was Bis' day, and as he returned with his crew from their three hour workout, all of them commented that after the initial exercise, it actually became fun, and everyone felt physically and mentally better for it.

Upon entering their barracks, Bis, who then headed for his semiprivate room and a good shower, was stopped by Corporal Tooley, who trying to be humorous, said, "Are you guys ready for the Olympics yet?" which, in the searing July heat, was met with blank stares. The Corporal, seeing it was not the time or place, then told Bis, "I was over at the Battalion talking to the First Sergeant. On the way back, I stopped at the Battalion Communication Room to pick up any stuff that might be in our box. While I was there, the Staff Major came in. He asked about you, and told me to have you report to him at ten hundred hours tomorrow, unless you have an official conflict."

"Is that all he said?" asked Bis.

Tooley nodded in the affirmative, as Bis, puzzled, continued on to his room.

Promptly at ten o'clock a.m., Bis, showered, shaved, and in a newly laundered uniform, presented himself to the Major's office.

The Major, obviously expecting Bis, was in the Brigade waiting room. He welcomed him upon his arrival, saying, "Come into my office."

After saluting, Bis was then asked to sit down. The Major cautioning, "Relax, I just want to go over some things with you."

Bis, concerned he might be in some sort of trouble, but such not being the case, did relax.

"I want to give you my personal congratulation on your actions in the recent Rashad affair. I am going to recommend to the Battalion Commander that he approve the awarding to you of the Silver Star," adding, "Most recipients don't deserve it. You do."

The Major continued, "The main reason I wanted to talk to you is, I want your permission for me to send in your application to be accepted as one of the new inductees, offered by the Battalion to the current Officer Candidate School. Slots have just opened up again, and it could not have come at a better time."

Bis smiled at the accolades, and then told the Major, "I appreciate all the recommendations, and also the interest you have shown in me. I don't really think the deeds done at Rashad were all that heroic, but if it will reflect well on the Stryker Battalion, so be it," adding, "Under all the circumstances, however, I will have to think about attending the Officer's Candidate School. Can you delay the application?"

"Why delay," the Major insisted.

"First, I want to decide whether I want to remain in the service as my professional goal. I have plenty of time served already, but I also have credentials as a professor of English Literature. Secondly, I have an obligation to my Stryker Squad to see them through this unpredictable period. There are serious doubts whether the Maliki Government can make it, and at the same time, whether the probable Sunni- Shi'ite instability, will put my Squad, along with all in Iraq American troops, in jeopardy, as Iraq returns to chaos. Add to that the dual problems of Afghanistan going to pot, and Israel pushing hard to talk the president and Congress into attacking Iran."

Bis continued, "Admiral Mike Mullen, Chairman of the Joint Chiefs, said it best, "That I am concerned, any

US, or Israeli strike on Iran carries a notable exposure to more risk in the Middle East - - - contributing - - - to possible unintended consequences, '" adding, "Iraq is also, basically, an Emir controlled nation, and governed by Shariah."

The Major had listened, intently, to Bis' remarks, and then responded, "The additional years you would have to remain in the US Army until you could retire are few, and you could then resume your teaching profession as a relatively young man. Knowing your ability, and what you have already accomplished as a Sergeant, you would be able to offer the Army some valuable insights, and open many doors, which as an officer, you could not before."

The Major continued, "As to the Maliki obstacles you mentioned, the slot does not take effect until February 15, 2009, which is, at least, seven months away. The time span will allow you to see what develops as to your troops concerns," adding, "You can, therefore, sign the application now, and, if something interceded, withdraw it, up until February 2009.

"You mentioned Shariah," the Major continued, "What can you tell me as to your understanding of that word, and also the Islamic word 'jihad'," adding, "I have my own thoughts, but I want to see how some other thoughtful person might perceive these strange, foreign words."

"Using me as a guinea pig, huh?" Bis laughed, but then replying, said, "Both words are serious, fateful, deeply active, and yet deceptive Muslim words. America, and the Western world, better ponder and consider those words carefully.

"The word 'Shariah', technically, is defined as a type of foundational law, or a kind of Islamic Constitution. It is the means that both Sunni and Shi'ite Emirs use to announce, and support, their transnational Islamic authority. It is the so-called law of all Islamic lands, and parts of this written law can be found in the Koran. It can also be transmitted by Emir issued fatwas. It is mainly a control mechanism. Through the use of Shariah, the Emirs dictate to all practicing Muslims, moderate or not, what they must believe, if they want to be considered good, faithful Muslims, including both Sunni and Shi'ite sects."

Bis continued, "Islam, as we both know, is not a religion, but is mainly a lifestyle. It is the way the Emir maintains this complete dominance over the individual Muslim's personal, social, family, military, and faith life. Under Shariah Law, whatever is necessary to give effect and to ensure complete submission to Islam, including murder, mayhem, assault, lying, or any other use of violent means, can be legally ordered by the Sunni or Shi'ite Emir. Shariah condones, and often requires, such barbaric practices as the beheading of any Muslim who turns from Islam to Christianity. It also is what is used to order the killing of Mid East Christians, as we have seen with the continuous slaughter of centuries old Chaldean, Iraqi Christians, condoned, merely by avoiding their eyes to it, by Bush and Petraeus. Shariah also prescribes stoning for female adulterers, but exempts men. It suggests flagellation for unchaste women, and legally allows genital mutilation to be administered to female children," adding, "But equal to all of Islam's un-religious, barbaric actions, Shariah's authorizing of individual Muslims, men, women, and children, to forfeit their lives, in various suicide assaults, is the worst. Giving Allah's assurance that those unfortunate souls, who give their lives that they will be martyred, is a bold faced lie. This jihad martyrdom only serves the political or military purposes or programs of the Emirs, or of a group of Emirs."

Bis then concluded, "Consideration of the other evil word, jihad, brings forth another factor in looking at Islam. This factor must also be considered as involved in the operation of Maliki's present Iraqi government. Jihad, in truth, is merely another control mechanism. It is the Emir's pronouncement to all Moslems of their conception of Islamic purity. It is hailed as the ultimate good and of the holy state which surrounds Islamic affairs. Jihad is what motivates all good Moslems to support Islam, no matter what. It is what Emirs use to justify their barbaric criminal activity. Also, it is what the Emirs consider imperitive, in Islam's ever-going war against unbelievers, and it is the religious excuse the Emirs use in justification of murder, assault, and mayhem against any who do not believe.

"It takes a person exercising total control, with no consciences, to unleash these evil forces, and then have the audacity, guts, or callousness to call those unholy actions a holy act, or a martyrdom act," adding, "The jihadist, fulfilling his evil, slimy, barbaric, murderous acts, most greater than other heinous acts depicted in history, is given a complete religious cover. The jihadist is smothered by the pure, thick, jihad holiness cloak, spread by their sponsoring Emir, while at the same time, the jihadist is doing the work of Lucifer."

Bis continued, "This holy conception of jihad, or what they consider Islamic purity, is also taught, and forms the basic framework of Islamic jurisprudence, in all Muslim schools, both Sunni and Shi'ite, including the Iraqi schools under Maliki's jurisdiction," adding, "But more ominously, this jihad purity is also taught in Moslem schools, operating with official blessing, in America, financed by Saudi Arabian oil money."

The Major was mesmerized, and had not moved. He had been totally entranced with Bis' unexpected tirade against Islam, and marveled at his total understanding, and thorough explanation of the words "Shariah" and "jihad". The Major throughout had not murmured a syllable, and in fact he had not even taken a long breath during the long Bis disclosure.

"Don't you agree, however, that Iraq will stumble back into a Sunni-Shi'ite chaos if the US leaves Iraq without making sure Maliki has complete control of the Iraqi military?" the Major finally blurted out.

"Chaos will happen, no matter what," offered Bis, adding, "Merely by saying Iraq is a democracy will not make it so. Iraq is really only a third class, poor, Middle East, Islamic entity, which cannot overcome the nonsensical, but centuries old war between Sunnis, who want a central caliphate, and the Shi'ites, who don't."

Bis continued, "The problem has never been America's problem, until the neo-cons and Israel dragged us into this unwinnable Islamic dilemma," adding, "As most of our discerning American generals have observed, the situations in Iraq and Afghanistan don't pose a strategic threat to America, unless they are somehow joined by a modern industrial nation-state. Our brainless lingering in Iraq could involuntarily actually create a threat."

Bis, shifted in his chair, re-crossed his legs and then asked, "Do you want me to continue my lecture?"

The Major smiled, but then paled and answered, "If the truth were known, if I had to testify under oath, I would have responses almost identical to yours. Please go on."

"There are two big problems," Bis replied, "The first is the brainless, suicidal, self-destruction of the US Army. Since Bush's invasion of Iraq in 2003, America's ground forces have, for the most part, virtually ended their usual maneuver training war games. In today's world, there are two potential enemies who could challenge America to a conventional war: China, particularly, and Russia, eventually, if the neo-cons and Israel, succeed in making Russia our mortal enemy. The US Army, since 2003, is built on, and trained for, only low intensity, small scale guerilla warfare. If it is suddenly called upon to defend a conventional war - - - ," Bis' voice trailed off.

The Major nodded in agreement, interceding, "It could be a major, strategic tragedy."

"The second suicidal self-destruct problem," Bis continued, "is the neo-con, Israeli, and congressional insistence that the US Armed Forces must go to war with Iran," adding, "If Iraq, by its stupidity, was able to bring the, previous to Bush, American super power to its knees and bankruptcy, such insane Iranian activity, will render America, and the American people absolutely prostrate."

Bis continued, "Iran never has been a strategic threat to either the US or Israel. By possessing a calculated two hundred major nuclear warheads, Israel is currently the top military dog in the Middle East, but it still wants to be the only nuclear dog, able to expand at will. General Zinni, General Abizaid, and Admiral Fallon, have all made clear, by public declarations, that to bomb Iran is insane and stupid, and potentially fatal to America," adding, "Bush and his neo-cons, in addition to urging an Iranian attack, have aided and abetted the kept American media in its lies. They all are constantly attacking the Iranian president, Ahmadinejad, as another Hitler, but what none of them tell America, is that he has no real control over Iran's nuclear situation. The Iranian constitution reserves nuclear decisions only to Iran's supreme religious leader, ali-Khamenei. He repeatedly has stated Iran wants only industrial nuclear power."

Bis continued, "What is even more ironic, and equally interesting, is that Ahmadinejad's opponent, former chief nuclear negotiator, ali-Larijani, has just been recently elected the new Speaker of the Iranian Parliament. This could not have happened without the quiet assent of ali-Khamenei," adding, "Larijani could well unseat Ahmadinejad in the upcoming 2009 general elections.

"More disgusting and disheartening," Bis pointed out, "is Bush and Petraeus' willingness to resort to fraud and trickery to convince the American people, and others, that Iran is providing arms and sustenance to Iraq's Shi'ite and Mahdi Army, and is actively engaged in meddling in Iraq's affairs.

"Both men intentionally plotted to advance a scheme that would publically expose what they called specific convicting documents, and also would produce actual Iranian heavy armament pieces, all intended to positively prove Iran was actively engaged in killing US soldiers," adding, "The plot failed and instead of providing detailed evidence of Iranian evil intentions, from the collection of arms that was supposedly collected from around the Iraqi Sadr City of Karbala, and included several mortars, anti-aircraft missiles, and roadside explosive devices, not a single one of these weapons was proven to be of Iranian origin despite the presence of the Sadr Mahdi Army in this same area for months. To make matters worse, a Maliki advisor, Haider Abadi, told the *Los Angeles Times*, which remained unreported, that Iranian officials had given Maliki substantial believable evidence that Iran, in fact, had not been involved. To cement the farce, when US munitions experts went to Karbala to examine the alleged weapons, they found nothing that could credibly link them to Iran."

Bis then pointed out, "As a result, Petraeus, embarrassed by the whole matter, had to cancel the planned US Press media event, which it had hoped would convict Iran. Maliki, himself, had to backtrack, and defensively appointed an Iraqi Committee to look into the origin of the Petraeus-Bush scheme, saying, 'speculation is not acceptable,'" adding, "The obvious implication that Petraeus-Bush had engaged in fraud and trickery was apparent. That it is being pushed by

Iraq's government is shameful, and a blow to America's honor."

Bis concluded, "To sum things up: promoting American interests by fraud will not go unnoticed in the world. Maliki's Iraqi government will eventually fracture, whether US troops are in Iraq or not. Maliki does not run Iraq. The Emirs run Iraq, and the Emirs, in turn, are controlled by the various ayatollahs, Sunni or Shi'ite. And lastly, America should not be in Iraq. Israel, the instigator, has only been weakened by its insistence on the invasion of Iraq and now of Iran," adding, "Overall, it would seem that current American and Israeli political leaders are following a death wish. It would also seem that a majority of the American electorate are brain dead."

Bis paused for a long minute, during which time the Major remained as in a stupor. The quiet between them was finally broken as Bis intoned, "Hand me the OCS application. I will sign it, on condition that I can withdraw it, if the situation warrants."

CHAPTER XVII – "AFGHANISTAN"

A week had gone by since Bis had given the Major his professorial lecture on the ups and downs of Iraq.

Bis also experienced misgivings about his signing the OCS application, but always reverted to the saving fact that he could withdraw it.

Bis did not tell Tooley, or anyone else, about the signed commitment. It was his and the Major's deep, dark secret.

While these matters weighed heavily on his mind, it was Afghanistan that was on Tooley's mind.

"I've been talking to the Brigade First Sergeant," the Corporal admitted, discussing the deep subject at a most unusual time, as he and Bis happened to be brushing their teeth.

"What did he say?"Bis, faking a strong interest, blurted out, spitting the brush residue from his mouth.

Tooley laughed, but continued, "He says in the next thirty days some US troops are going to be willingly, or not, transferred from Iraq to Afghanistan," adding, "Probably engineers, mine disposal troops, and few other support people."

Continuing the thought as they walked back to their uncozy cots, Bis pointed out, "Just like it is in Iraq, the Afghan guy the neo-cons picked to front for them in Afghanistan, President Hamid Karzai, is weak, ineffective, and corrupt. He and the neo-cons are causing the nation to fall back into the hands of the Taliban."

Tooley nodded, and then related, "The First Sergeant also told me that the poor US taxpayers, since September 11, 2001, have been stuck with thirty billion dollars in direct aid paid to Karzai cronies, plus ten billion dollars in promised aid, all of which doesn't seem to help the common Afghan folks, but certainly brightens up the day for the already rich, and powerful, Afghan warlords."

Bis smiled, and intoned, "Your Brigade First Sergeant is a veritable encyclopedia of facts and figures, but this time he is right. Karzai's brother, Wali Karzai, for one, publicly, obviously, and without embarrassment, receives protection and bribe money from known drug lords located in various parts of Afghan, with no state interference, all of which facilitate easy drug movement in and out of Afghanistan," adding, "Karzai also, recently, when given an opportunity to arrest a particularly bad, indiscriminate murderer, and war lord, Abdul Rasid Dostum, refused to do so, claiming the guy was too powerful. Karzai admittedly feared for his own life. So much for sovereignty."

"Like you said, going to Afghanistan from Iraq may be like jumping from the frying pan," Tooley admitted, "into the fire, but my encyclopedic First Sergeant friend did say, in thrity days hence, there will be a Brigade, now stationed in Iraq, transferred to Afghanistan. Things are getting rough in Karzai country."

"Did he say whether it was a Stryker Brigade?" Bis asked. "Did he say whether it was a voluntary Brigade?"

"Next time," Tooley ventured, "I'm going to take you with me," laughing, but looking deadly serious, at the same time.

Another three days quickly passed as both Bis and Tooley valiantly tried to keep tabs on any Afghan goings on, but there was no reliable scuttlebutt regarding any Stryker Brigade transfers to Afghanistan. The thought was, however, constantly on their minds and on the minds of their fellow squadmen.

Bis decided to ask for advice from one, who he considered a fountainhead of information in Iraq, his friend, the Brigade Staff Major. If he did not know, it did not exist.

Bis contacted the Major, and made arrangements to see him at his office, alone, on Saturday, an unusual time, July 28, 2008.

At the appointed time, the Major, for security's sake, manned the front door of the Brigade Communication Building, thereafter using his keys to usher both of them to the Major's office, relocking each door they had opened.

"Must be important, Sergeant," the Major intoned, smiling.

"It is to me," Bis admitted, after first taking the offered seat in the usual chair in front of the Major's desk.

"I consider you, not only as a commanding officer, but also as a friend I can confide in," Bis volunteered. "The Iraq-Afghan Brigade transfers, which are on everybody's mind, are also on mine. I would like to get a handle on the truth, and whether the 711th Stryker Battalion is in jeopardy of being involuntarily deployed to Afghanistan."

"I figured that would be the crux of this discussion," the Major responded.

The Major continued, "I will give you all the information I have. It is because I consider you a good friend, and as one the few loyal Americans in Iraq, I can confide in with relevant facts, and know that they will not leave this room."

He continued, "About fifteen hundred Marines now stationed in Afghanistan have had their tours extended for at least thirty days, maybe more. The Marines have taken it on the nose lately, four were killed recently in Kandahar, a city and also a province in southwestern Afghanistan, by roadside bombs," adding, "The loss of these highly trained security Marines has caused a high level decision to immediately deploy two to three hundred security support troops from Iraq to Afghanistan, including up to eight helicopter crews."

"But no Stryker Brigades, as yet?" Bis questioned.

The Major shook his head no, and then offered, "You are aware that back in the middle of June, several dozen Taliban terrorists on motor bikes, in a well planned synchronized attack, stormed Afghan guards at Kandahar's well known prison, Sarposa. They used a suicide tanker truck full of explosives to blow down and destroy the main prison gate, and a second suicide tanker truck, a few minutes later, blasted an escape route through the prison's back wall. Several security troops were killed, and eight hundred seventy inmates from the prison, easily escaped," adding, "Of those escaping, three hundred ninety were Taliban prisoners."

"Sounds like the CIA or the FBI could not have planned it better," Bis offered, shaking his head in disbelief.

"The American military has invested a lot of time, money, and men in capturing those Taliban prisoners," the Major intoned. "They had been interned, and interred in Kandahar at the insistence of the Karzai folks, even though Kandahar was the Taliban's former stronghold, and has been the scene of fierce fighting the last several years between American troops and the Taliban."

"Sounds like a set up," Bis interposed.

"One of the prison's chief officials has been detained for complicity," the Major responded. "The Taliban, conveniently, also had several cars waiting outside the blown up back wall, to whisk away the Taliban escapees, making it obvious the break was given a lot of inside help. Its execution was a piece of cake," adding, "Only ten miles northwest of Kandahar City is a place called the Arghandah Valley, which is one of the few lush agricultural sites in Afghanistan. It is filled with grape and pomegranate groves. The Taliban have virtually taken over this area. It is also estimated by the locals that about five hundred Taliban fighters have taken up residence in the valley. Many families are fleeing the area and allowing the terrorists to take over several of the local villages. They, in effect, operate as a shadow government, working as farmers during the day, and switching to Taliban fighters at night."

The Major continued, "The Taliban superstructure in the Arghandah Valley area has completely taken over the existing cell phone network. They put out the word, after they had blown up a few telephone towers, insisting that the cell phone companies must cease and restrict phone coverage between 5:00 p.m. and 7:00 a.m. each day, or there would be bad consequences. The companies have done as the terrorists have demanded."

"Wow," Bis exclaimed. "You can see where the power is."

Nodding his head in agreement, the Major interposed, "Karzai's government can't stop them. The GI's can't stop them. NATO can't stop them."

"Looks like we got real troubles," Bis offered. "Right there in River City," smiling, "I mean Kandahar River City."

Bis continued, "When Afghanistan is properly considered, it is one of the most mountainous, least hospitable places in the world, almost the equal of

Tibet. When a few hundred of our special operation troops were first deployed into Afghanistan, after the September 11, 2001, New York attack, and we discovered an al-Qaeda connection, it was only to try to destroy al-Qaeda, and to dispose of the entrenched Taliban. There was no major American policy of bringing neo-con democracy to that poor nation," adding, "Within a few months, our special troops gained all of their objectives, except capturing bin Laden, and probably could have gotten him, if given their head."

"The Bush Administration's decision to then withdraw those troops, and send them into an Iraqi invasion was a mistake," The Major offered.

"Not only a mistake," Bis responded, "but a strategic mistake. The lack of our attention allowed the Taliban to then re-group. They have since rebuilt their army through tribal recruits taken from the three million Afghan-Pakistan Moslems living in the unapproachable, ungovernable tribal regions located in the outer areas of mountainous Pakistan, where the Taliban are not only welcomed, but protected by the Pakistan government."

Bis continued, "When Bush decided to democratize Afghanistan, to bring President Hamid Karzai to power, he also decided to bring in NATO Forces, and to compliment them with infusions of regular US Forces, including training troops," adding, "That's when the whole thing fell apart."

"The war in Afghanistan is not regular, but is irregular warfare," the Major agreed, nodding, "The topography of the country requires that reasonable aims would dictate the use of special operation troops only. We can't expect to take and hold ground, so the neo-cons can come in and try to democratize it."

Bis, surprised at the Major's assertion, interposed, "You are right. Taliban, or al-Qaeda, strongholds should be hit hard by airstrikes, and quick moving Marines, Green Berets, or Navy Seals. To depend on NATO troops in a fight situation, is to concede the fight," adding, "Look at our NATO allies, Germany, France, and Italy. They would not let their troops engage in any armed battles, which not only makes them useless, but is a great danger to American troops. Countries that do contribute fighting troops, for strictly political reasons, refuse to bring in any additional troops to assist our GI's."

"Of the fifty-two thousand NATO troops now in Afghanistan, thirty thousand of them are American," the Major commented, adding, "When Bush includes NATO, the US contingent, itself, can no longer make the necessary decisions, you must then reach a consensus."

"Which is impossible," Bis asserted. "Both presidential candidates are now calling for an Afghan surge, joined by the weak kneed generals put in charge by Bush and his neo-cons. More troops will probably worsen problems in that unfortunate nation, now fractured in several parts and controlled and operated by sectional war lords."

Bis continued, "The Taliban, like the al-Qaeda, and others in Iraq and Afghanistan, who want us out, use their main talking point that their nations are being, in fact, occupied by the great Satans, Israel and

America. What are their biggest and most effective offensive weapons?"

In answer to his own question, Bis blurted out, "Suicide bombers, and self-exploding roadside bombs made from old artillery shells," adding, "For these to be effective, drug induced suicide bombers, anxious to be martyred, need many troops, and a lot of machines gathered in one spot, or in long lines of vulnerable Humvees, to succumb to roadside bombs."

Shaking his head, up and down, in agreement, the Major pointed out, "Fighter planes with laser bombs, pinpointing Taliban strongholds. Helicopter flying low and then emerging with their .50 caliber machine guns blasting, knocking the unsuspecting terrorists off their feet. A swoop into the un-expectant Taliban headquarters, with a platoon of specialty trained, specialty armed Marines or Berets, moving quickly out, leaving behind an enemy cemetery. These are the most effective military means to blast the Taliban back to the unknown."

"The locals, also, with only small specialty GI's, don't see lots of troops marching, or of forces building the occupying barracks in their villages, which ignites the jihadist souls of both the Sunnis and the Shi'ites," Bis commented. "When the Marines, a few months ago, established a permanent observation base on a remote mountaintop on the Afghan-Pakistan border, it merely invited the Taliban to attack it, which they did, killing nine Marines, and wounding fifteen. It is a good example of trying to occupy."

"They have since closed it down, which was the proper thing to do," the Major replied.

"All the troops injured in the attack were American," Bis offered, "not a single NATO," adding, "My assessment is if the Pentagon continued to back the Bush-neo-con decision to add three new Brigades to Afghanistan, to back up their impossible Israeli dream of making that nation an accommodating democracy, it will fail. Any policy which requires a Western occupation of a Muslim nation will fail."

Bis continued, "Common sense blares out that it would be stupid to put a wheeled Stryker Battalion into a place where there are no extensive roads of any kind, only remote back trails which lead to no where in Afghanistan. But that does not mean it will not happen."

"Your judgment and my judgment, on this point, are the same," the Major admitted, adding, "I will recommend against it, but that will not be controlling. Sorry I can't give you a more definitive answer."

"You answered more questions than you think," Bis responded, standing to salute the Major, "That is why I have respect for you."

As Bis and the Major left the room, the Major gave Bis this respectful reply, "I would rather talk to you about things in Iraq or Afghanistan than to the colonels or generals. You make more sense."

CHAPTER XVIII – SADR CITY REVISITED

Bis, not wanting to inadvertently disclose any information the Major had given him, did not talk to any of his squadmen, including Tooley, when he returned to his barracks.

Tooley, not really knowing that Bis had spent the morning with the Major, instead woke Bis from a catnap, saying, "I just talked to the Brigade Sergeant. He said the Brigade got an update from the Pentagon about the new US Military Commander of NATO forces in Afghanistan. His name is General Dave McKiernan. True to form, he chants the same old NATO mantra, saying the International Security Assistance Force, which is the NATO mandate, does not extend across the border into Pakistan."

He continued, "The First Sergeant and I discussed the fact that, time and time again, Afghanistan has fooled Bush into thinking the Afghans were our bosom buddy allies, when each time they double-crossed us, in fact, first by their inaction against cross border attacks on American troops in Afghanistan, and second by closing their eyes to Pakistanis joining the Taliban terrorist army."

"But at the same time," Bis interposed, "the Afghans, who run this phony, one city government, collect billions of US taxpayer dollars, a gift from Bush and the Congress, for such perfidy," adding, "The new commander still keeps the fatal mindset that NATO military operations cannot be conducted in so-called sovereign Pakistan Territory, where the Taliban problems are."

"The First Sergeant also says, the Pentagon thinks they can find enough smaller units, such as engineering and aviation surveillance troops, to quiet the ever louder demands for more troops from the American commanders on the ground," Tooley responded. "Oh, by the way, our Squadron Captain has been designated as the representative battalion officer to attend an Afghan briefing by the Pentagon. For media image purposes, they have set up the conference tomorrow, July 29, 2008, at the new Iraqi Communications Building, near the three mile US, newly installed and hated, cement wall, in good, old Sadr City."

Bis, with this news, sat up from his cot, saying, "I don't like that. It could be a catastrophic invitation to hit the conference with suicide bombers, or roadside bombs. It could be done, by either Sunnis or Sadr Shi'ites."

"The conference must be well protected," Tooley commented. "They surely realize the importance of the meeting. I'm certain the Maliki government has put their best troops on guard."

"I would not trust any Iraqi government troops, especially in a situation where it could really embarrass the US," Bis replied. "These Moslems, or all sects, Sunnis or Shi'ites, are first of all, anti-Christian, and then anti-American."

Bis continued, "This resurrected Muslim self-hate seems to have reached its Zenith in Iraq and Afghanistan, and other Moslem nations, coinciding with the American-Israeli invasion, and occupation, of Iraq. I have talked to many Iraqis, Christians and Muslims, and they tell me, when they grew up in Baghdad, there was no reference among their neighbors as to who was a Jew, who was a Christian, or who was a Sunni or Shi'ite, until the 2003 invasion," adding, "You can also see the neo-con inspired occupying effect in Egypt. Since the US invasion, one hundred fifty thousand Iraqis have sought refuge in Egypt. That nation is now engaged in trying to control, not only anti-Christian killings and outbreaks, but serious fighting among the Sunnis and the Shi'ites."

Tooley interposed, "There are now, as a result of US interference, two million refugee Iraqis around the Muslim world, and the same Sunni hates Shi'ite problem is occurring in Lebanon," adding, "The problem is made even worse for innocent Iraqi Christians, trying to find security in order to practice their Christianity by fleeing the American tacitly approved killing of their 2000 year old Christian-Coptics, by the Maliki government. The hatred goes ahead of them to Egypt."

"It does not help matters," Bis responded, "that Egypt's president, Hosni Mubarak, a Sunni, recently remarked, "Shi'ites are more loyal to Iran than to Egypt," adding, "The point is, the US-Israeli-neo-con objective of gaining control of the Muslim world by creating so-called friendly democratization, along with its attending occupation, has created a worldwide crisis, disrupted the Middle East into an unrecognizable state of affairs, destroyed the centuries old Christian Arab enclaves, and discredited and bankrupted America into an atmosphere of ever growing Muslim hatred."

"Yet," Tooley pointed out, "NATO continued to press for more money for so-called economic and humanitarian aid in Afghanistan. They blame the newly rising Taliban threat on the American policy of trying to eradicate the poppy-drug problems, rather than Moslem hate."

"You notice that the NATO spokesmen are always referring to US taxpayer aid, not to monies coming from the European Union," Bis contended, chuckling.

Bis added, "The continuing brainless, Bush neo-con-Israeli position is that Afghanistan is deteriorating and needing more democratization. New American blood and US taxpayer substance is their solution. At the same time, that war with Iran is absolutely necessary and desirable."

"Did you see where the Democrats in Congress," Tooley murmured, "led by New York Representative, Gary Ackerman, who, along with some Republicans, led by newly converted neo-con, Mike Pence of

Indiana, are pushing for House Concurrent Resolution 362, which demands a complete Iranian blockade of imports and exports. It is, in effect, a declaration of war."

"Israel is fully backing that resolution, along with AIPAC," Bis noted, "To enact it, would be a tragedy," adding, "The Congress has again failed to comprehend, and the media has failed to report to the American people, two very important recent disclosures. One, that the National Intelligence Estimate, a combination of several US intelligence groups, has confirmed that Iran ceased trying to establish a nuclear weapons agenda way back in 2003. Secondly, the liberals own Under-secretary of State, Nick Burns, has recently admitted that, 'Iran has not yet perfected uranium enrichment,' explaining Iran does not have the knowledge to even convert uranium gas into fuels for use in power plants, let alone to build bombs. He pointed out, even if some day she can learn to enrich to weapons grade, Iran would still have to create and test a useable nuclear weapon, and then try to devise a way to deploy it," adding, "With these facts, it is clear, Bush, Israel, and the neo-cons are lying to America. They are falsifying facts, like they did with Iraq, as an excuse to get us into a war with Iran. That such a war would be devastating to America, the whole Middle East and to Israel itself, does not seem to matter."

"You would think that Israel would understand, if America goes, they go," Tooley intoned, adding, "When you consider Israeli history, the same bullheaded stupidity cost them their Israel homeland two thousand years ago, and again three thousand years ago."

The following morning, Tooley reported back to Bis the details he got from the Brigade First Sergeant, as to the Captain's itinerary, and also his times of departure and return, saying, "The Captain, along with officers from the other Stryker Brigades will exit the Green Zone at 0500 hours, in a convoy of five Humvees, with a Bradley in front, and in the rear. They will proceed, posthaste, straight to the center of the three mile, twenty foot tall, cement wall, put up by the troops two months ago. Iraqi troops, also with Bradleys and Humvees, will meet and escort them from a point outside of Sadr City to the new Iraqi Communications Building, near the center of the cement barrier in Sadr City."

"Did he say, exactly where the Iraqi's would intersect them?" Bis asked, looking anxiously.

"Only at about 0600 hours on the 29th day of July, 2008, and at a point outside of Sadr City," Tooley replied, "Why are you so concerned about that?"

Bis said nothing, but nursing a hunch, that the details, and the placing of the Afghan Conference, would not go unnoticed by Sadr Shi'ite forces, or anti-American Sunni forces. It was a feeling deep in his gut that would not go away.

Bis slept fitfully that night, waking several times. He finally succumbed into a deep slumber that lasted 'til 6:30 a.m., when Tooley woke him, saying, "Bis, one of the Brigade's Humvees just pulled back into headquarters with the tragic news that it and a Bradley were the only survivors of an ambush on the Stryker officer's convoy. I happened to hear the racket and ran over there. I heard the Humvee driver say he was the last Humvee in the convoy, and watched in horror as the Bradley heading them up, along with the next three Humvees, suddenly flew up in the air, the doors flapping open like a pair of wings. He said the turret gunners were shot out of their canisters like Roman candles," adding, "The roadside bombs must have contained huge amounts of explosives, leaving gigantic holes in the streets and sidewalks, and causing lesser damage to some of the other vehicles."

"What about the Captain?" Bis asked. "What happened to him?"

"I asked them about that," Tooley replied. "The Humvee driver said one Humvee was severely damaged, but not destroyed, and the occupants got out and ran back to the two trucks, which were also not damaged. One other Humvee, which I think was the Captain's, was rolled on its side, and then catapulted end over end, into a deep, previous, explosion made cavern, landing top down. The driver said he did not see anyone come out of that Humvee. The other two Humvees, along with the leading Bradley, were blown apart and scattered."

"Didn't they go down and check?" Bis asked, shaking his head in disbelief.

"The driver said that after the initial bombing, which began with a metallic sound, like a rock hitting a barrel, followed by the most unbelievable explosions, the Iraqi troops, who had just joined the convoy a few minutes earlier, and took positions at the head of the convoy, took off. When the explosions took place, they, to a man, ran. They just kept heading down the road."

"Looks like the bombs were calculated, and set off by probable Sadr terrorists by remote control," Bis claimed. "Obviously they waited until the Iraqi troops passed the blow up point before they set them off."

"The Humvee driver said the terrorists came from nowhere, and everywhere, and in unbelievable numbers. They surrounded the blown up Bradley and the three destroyed Humvees, left in various positions on the road. They continued to shoot at them, pumping thousands of rounds from their AK-47's. The US troops, except for the third Humvee who escaped, were already dead from the bombings. The terrorists were not able to get into position to shoot at the Captain's Humvee because it was protected by the level of the roadway."

Bis, at that information, lit up like the Fourth of July, saying, "Since the terrorists could not destroy the Humvee, maybe the Captain survived," adding, "It's a long shot, but it would be a worthy long shot."

Bis pondered the situation for a minute, and then told Tooley, "Come on. We are going hunting."

As Tooley followed Bis to the Battalion Communication Building, Bis asked, "How did the firefight end? What happened to the terrorists?"

"The Humvee driver said that all the survivors joined forces in a concentrated M-4 rifle fire ring, which was evidently effective, and the terrorists disappeared as quickly as they appeared. It was also then getting light and they faded back into their Sadr neighborhood," Tooley responded, adding, "The surviving US troops hightailed it back to the Green Zone."

By that time, the two were walking into the communication building, and Bis was asking permission to see the Major, which was quickly granted by the officer manning the Officer-of-the-Day post.

Bis and Tooley saluted as they entered the Major's office, and Bis got right to the point, saying, "Sir, it is now 0800 hours, or about two hours since the Captain's convoy was ambushed. The surviving Humvee has told us that our Captain's Humvee was catapulted into a kind of a ravine, landing on its top, but the terrorists were not able to throw any secondary fire into it. The witness also said no one appeared on the ground around the Humvee after the crash, and that no terrorists were able to molest the wreckage. The survivors also said they left the scene without checking the Captain's vehicle."

"What's on your mind?" the Major responded.

"The Captain deserves to have his body brought back," Bis acknowledged, "and stranger things have happened. He might still be alive. No one has confirmed he is dead," adding, Tooley and I have made several trips to the Sadr City area earlier, and we know the territory.

"I want permission for our 7th Squadron, and also the 3rd Squadron, to provide us cover, while Tooley and I check the Captain's Humvee, and either bring back his body, or hopefully get him to the medics," Bis continued, "We have to do it now. We have to do it before the terrorists get to him."

"How do you know, Sergeant that the Battalion CO is gone for a few days, and I am acting commander?" smiled the Major, adding, Permission is granted, that is if you don't run into another ambush. If you do, then you must abort the mission."

The Major continued, "How do you know the 3rd Squadron will join you?"

"They will, Sir," answered Bis, saluting, as he and Tooley left the office, hurrying back to their barracks.

"Thank you for volunteering me to check out the Captain's Humvee," Tooley laughed. "I guess you knew I would do it even without asking," adding, "What about the 3rd, do you want me to get them ready?"

Bis nodded, and interposed, "I'm going to call the Stryker pool and tell our drivers to bring both Strykers to the barracks, and be ready to go by 0900 hours."

At precisely 0930 hours, about three-and-a-half hours after the ambush, Bis and Tooley, along with his 7th Stryker Rifle Squad, aided by the 3rd Stryker Rifle Squad, along with their vehicles, arrived at the explosion area. Tooley, before they left the Green Zone, came across the driver from the surviving Humvee vehicle, who anxiously volunteered to direct the Stryker group back to the correct spot.

Once there, Bis clearly remembered the bleak street from previous trips to Sadr City, along with its bomb evacuated, secluded two block area. The semi-hidden, unique, extensive bomb crater, that the Captain and his Humvee had disappeared into, was obvious.

Bis, after viewing the situation, ordered his Stryker driver to position itself sidewise, partially over the edge of the road. He then asked his M-240 gunner, stationed on top, if he could see anything. "I see the axel, wheel, and part of the undercarriage of a Humvee," the gunner replied.

"Any sign of life, or evidence that the terrorists have riddled the Humvee carcass?" Bis asked.

"Nope. Nope. It looks quiet," was the reply.

Ding, ding, came new sounds, as Bis ordered the gunner to take cover, and motioning Tooley to come forward.

While the Corporal was doing so, Bis radioed the Sergeant commanding the 3rd Stryker, saying, "We are getting sniper fire. Probably from that line of buildings, one block to the west. I'm going to release a few smoke bombs between us and the buildings, and put my Squad behind the protecting Stryker, where they, and the M-240 gunner can combine and rake the area through the smoke," adding, "I hope you can do the same."

"Will do," answered the Sergeant.

"In five minutes, or 0945 hours, I will loose my smoke bombs, and then lead my Squad in place," Bis interposed. "Can you do the same? Our combined fire would be effective."

"Will do," returned the Sergeant. "Don't worry, we will also keep an eye on you, down in that hole."

By 0955, the smoke bombs were doing their jobs, and while a few terrorist bullets could be heard from time to time, the firepower from the M-4's and the

M-240 machine guns kept the enemy's head down, along with his AK-47's.

"Okay Corporal, lets go," Bis blurted, after handing the ends of two ropes to two squadmen, telling them, "This is to pull us out quickly if need be. It is also to be used to pull the Captain, or his body, and that of his driver, out of this miserable hole."

Scrambling, almost falling several times, Bis and Tooley, in their armor, with the ropes tied to them, with their M-4's plus ammo, cumbersomely made their way down the steep slopes leading to the overturned Humvee.

Tooley reached the area above the driver's door first, and down on his knees, crawled partially into that compartment.

"The driver is obviously dead," Tooley yelled. "The bomb just about blew him apart," adding, "I can't see into the back seat. There are several map cases, and other document cases the Captain must have brought with him."

"Pull the driver out. Let's get him pulled up and out of the way," Bis responded. "The driver's door is the only practical way into the Humvee."

Bis and Tooley labored hard to secure the driver's body on a flat piece of metal strewn from the wrecked Humvee, and tied one of the ropes to its end.

Bis yelled up the order to pull to the squadmen on the other end, screaming through the M-4 racket.

As the rope grew taunt, and began to lift its unfortunate burden, suddenly, from the opposite side of the depression, Bis heard the unmistakable sound of a sniper's bullet, which whistled close past his right ear, yelling, "Take cover."

Tooley automatically fell behind a mound of rock and dirt, asking in a loud voice, "Where?"

As Bis dove in behind Tooley, he pointed up and to the east. Just over the lip of the hole could be seen the roof of a three story building, three blocks to the east.

"Ah, yes," the Corporal responded. "I think I see a glint of a rifle barrel," adding, "I've got more room over here, let me give it a try, aiming his M-4 toward where he thought the sniper might be.

"Your eyes are better than mine," Bis intoned. "I can't see a thing."

"Shh," cautioned Tooley, as he mounted his M-4 on a handy rock.

A crucial minute went by, before the sniper fired again, sending his bullet to hit harmlessly, in the short space between Bis and the Corporal.

"I can see the spot," Tooley exclaimed, as he let go with three separate bursts from his M-4.

"I think I got him," the Corporal shouted. "I saw what looked like a rifle slide off the roof."

"I hereby award you the Annie Oakley prize," Bis shouted, adding, "I still did not see a thing. Cover me. I'm going to go into the Humvee."

Tooley watched as Bis exposed himself, confident he had vanquished the assailant.

Bis move unmolested into the back top area of the overturned vehicle, yelling, "These document cases show signs of stopping a lot of shrapnel. Could be a good omen.

"I found the Captain," Bis then exclaimed. "He is not moving, but he does not appear to be blown apart like the driver. The cases protected him."

Bis, with great exertion, began to work the Captain's dead weight toward the door, finally getting the head and one arm in a position where Tooley could help pull.

As he did, the Corporal stood up, elated, screaming, "I heard a moan. He's alive! He's alive!"

Every one of the Strykers took time out from the rifle barrages, as they each did little jigs, and exchanged high fives.

Bis beamed, as he and Tooley affixed the Captain to a scrap metal slide, tied to the squadmen on top, saying, "God and Christ were with us. I wish I could think of an appropriate remark from my heroes in American Literature, but my mind is blank."

"Amen," Tooley affirmed Bis' prayer, adding, "I have an appropriate remark from one of my heroes."

"Neil Armstrong said, 'Every human has a finite number of heartbeats. I don't intend to waste any of mine.'"

Bis laughed in agreement as he watched the Captain slowly being pulled out of perdition.

CHAPTER XIX –
THOUGHTS ALONG
THE TIGRIS

July 29, 2008 had been a long, grueling, but significant day in the lives of the 7th Squadron, the 3rd Squadron, and the remaining officers and men of the 7th Stryker Cavalry Regiment. They had their Stryker Captain back. He was badly, and sadly, wounded, but with an eighty percent chance of a full recovery. The close knit Regiment also now had valid bragging rights to their often made claim that they take care of their own, dead or alive.

Last, but certainly not least, was the obvious pride of the Regiment in their humble, professorial 7th Squadron Sergeant, who had so intelligently, and heroically, handled, not only the Stryker victory at Rashad earlier, but the daring rescue of their captain. The turn of events quashed any overt displeasure anyone might have harbored, to award the Silver Star to Bis.

Bis, however, was oblivious to the plaudits. Tooley was the Stryker, who, on his own, spread the "Bis is a hero" word, far and wide. If it were up to him, Bis would be awarded the Medal of Honor.

More interested in the fate of his Squadron, and what the Stryker Brigade's odds were to get out of Iraq whole, and avoid going to Afghanistan, was the topic most on Bis' mind.

To get away from his adoring fans, Bis decided to retreat to his known, quiet, get-away place. That part of the Tigris River which flowed within the Green Zone was one of the few spots where Bis could find some solitude, and then only late in the afternoon when merciful shade from the buildings lining this part of the river could keep the raging sun, and its overbearing heat, tolerable.

Bis, finally alone, leaned back against a sometime wooden fence, built askew along the riverbank, and blissfully rested his body, and his soul.

He watched the ever moving dirty water wend its way to the Persian Gulf, and finally relaxed, but his mind was on other things, *"America really only gets in war troubles when a president wants to make a mark on history, or to satisfy a particular constituency. The Congress, at times, can also be a willing conspirator. Usually, neither takes into account what the vast, middle class American thinks or feels about the issues, though these are the Americans who pay for our wars, both in lives, and in treasure."*

Bis shifted his backside forward to compensate for a disagreeable unsitable spot in the sand and rock, and continued his thinking, *"It was Kennedy who got*

America committed to the Viet Nam War. However, Lyndon Johnson greatly expanded it in August 1964, when an overwhelming Democrat Congress authorized unconstrained military forces to confront the Viet Cong in Viet Nam."

Bis continued thinking, *"The Viet Cong, however, began to be overtly supported by communist China and communist Russia, which sobered up the Democrat president, and Congress. The war was becoming, in their view, a political liability. In fact, it was,"* Bis reasoned, *"when Richard Nixon won the presidency in 1968, even though the US military had performed beautifully in 1968, culminating with what was called, 'The Tet Offensive', a victory over the Viet Cong and the North Vietnamese militarily. The media viewed it differently, however, and labeled it, falsely, as a defeat."*

Bis paused to breath a rare fresh gust of air, and to shift to a more comfortable position. Retaining his train of thought, he facetiously remembered a macabre Joe Stalin quote, *"'That a single death is a tragedy; a million deaths is a statistic,'"* continuing this thought about Viet Nam, Bis told himself, *"It was the very same Democrat Congress which authorized the Viet Nam War in 1964, and though America had a solid military victory, this did not alter their partisan thoughts. Now, they reasoned, there was a Republican president running the war, so the said Democrat Congress, in 1973, enacted a law making it unlawful for the president to expend treasury funds for combat anywhere in Indochina. The law gave an undeserved victory to the communist tyrant, Mao Tse-tung. The*

Congress, in effect, turned their back on the sacrifice of fifty-eight thousand American troops, who had died under their tutelage."

Bis shuttered visibly as he also remembered, *"That congressional slight of hand also cost the lives of hundreds of thousands of Vietnamese who had trusted in Kennedy and Johnson's words. While, at the same time in Cambodia, the Viet Nam defeat allowed a tyrant by the name of Pol Pot to come to rule. Under his hand one point seven million Cambodians were slaughtered, twenty percent of the population. Pol Pot, as the maniac he was, refused to use bullets in his massacres, and murdered those innocent people using axes, knives, and bamboo sticks. Children were simply battered against trees."*

Bis reached for his water bottle, thinking, *"These elite American empire builders, who take us to war, never seem to pay a price. It is always the insignificant, poor, innocent slob."*

Bis settled into a new posture, and continued his war thoughts, telling himself, *"This present war in Iraq is no different than the Viet Nam War. This time the elite war mongers are the neo-cons who want, above all, to protect Israel, and American interests be damned."*

He continued thinking, *"Their front man, General David Petraeus, continues to mouth the Bush-neo-con-Israeli propaganda line. Just a few days ago, Petraeus gave an interview to the American media, where he complemented probably the most neo-con-ish, phony, Iraqi ambassador ever, Ryan Cocker, describing him, 'I can just not imagine a better diplomatic wingman*

- - - we were determined to achieve unity of effort.'"
Bis laughed, *"What does he mean by that? Or when
he was quoted as saying, 'We've been at moments of
strategic change. These are not light switch moments
- - - what you have is more of a rheostat - - - many
rheostat moments - - - where in small areas, local
areas, districts and eventually provinces there is an
ongoing transition and has been an ongoing transition
for the Iraqi forces to step more into the lead and the
coalition forces to step back and provide enablers.'*

"What does that mean?" Bis asked himself. *"It is
nothing but a bunch of, I don't know when, if ever, that
the Maliki government will be able to take control.
This after five years of Iraqi empire building, and five
thousand American GI dead, and at a cost of one
trillion dollars.*

*"Petraeus continued with what is really a bunch
of bullshit. The same no meaning mish-mash, Bush,
and his helpers have been throwing at the unknowing
American public for years, saying, 'It is incremental.
It is this exercise of pushing the stone up the hill, a
Sisyphean endeavor at times where you do make two
steps up and one step back. Sometimes you make
one step up and two steps back,' or in other words, no
progress is being made. We are wasting our money and
our lives in Iraq."*

Bis laughed, recalling Petraeus' closing statement,
*"'Our objectives for 2009 – are a country that is at
peace with itself and its neighbors; a government
representative of and responsive to its people; a
productive member of the region and the global
economy,' an impossible goal. In the Middle East, it*

has been an ever impossible goal since Mohammad founded Islam, fourteen hundred years ago. Bush and company have, as their main occupation, the art of trying to fool the American citizen."

Bis continued thinking, *"Bush and Maliki in the last few days hinted that they might reach an agreement to satisfy the end of the year, expiring UN Mandate, supposedly they would pull US forces out of Iraqi cities by June of 2009, with all US combat forces out by 2010, and the remaining support troops out by 2012, but such a remedy is by no means certain. There remains, however, no agreement on immunity from prosecution for US soldiers under Iraqi law."* Bis laughed to himself, thinking, *"The no immunity problem should tell you something."*

Bis, with great effort in the debilitating heat, stood up, and moved to a shadier spot, with his attention suddenly drawn to the other side of the Tigris as he watched a group of adolescent Iraqi boys playing, and throwing rocks at the river's flow, thinking, *"At least that has not changed in the world."*

Settled in a new position, Bis continued his thoughts on Iraq, Islam, and its continuing effect on America, telling himself, *"The problem had its beginning with the speech made to a joint session of Congress by George H.W. Bush on September 1, 1990, when the president joined forces with the ancient and accepted Order of Jacobism, that monster of the French Revolution, by announcing his elation at the advent of the 'New World Order'. This supposed blessing, to be administered to mankind by the dominant international institutions, would result in peace and world prosperity. Super groups, like the United Nations, the European Union, and the superstructure of the defense organization, NATO, all controlled by elite one-worlders, considered themselves to be anointed with a never fail concept of continuing collective actions fulfilling their one world dreams. Most of us regular citizens are much more anxious, however, to reclaim and rebuild longstanding sovereign traditions, centuries old individual nations, and tribal nationalities. Bill Clinton's insane bombing war against Serbian nationalism provides an example of how the elite brainlessly endeavor to destroy centuries old Serb national tribal aspirations. Clinton used NATO to try to establish a so-called multicultural democracy on the Serbs. The multi-ethnic, multi-religious use of the collective order mechanism was a staple of Bush's 'New World Order'.*

"The Serbs did not take too kindly to Clinton and his NATO ally bombing them to kingdom come in Kosovo. At the same time, Clinton allowed criminal, Albanian war lords to invade Kosovo, and to destroy Serbian homes, and churches. A general genocide was inflicted on the Serbian population, who only wanted to continue to live in their Serbian Kosovo, sporting a long history of Serbian control and tradition. Serbia, along with Kosovo, is and was the Christian European nation, historically, which brought the Ottoman brand of militant Islam to a halt, short of Europe, centuries ago. As such, Serbia is known in the history books as the 'Guardians of the Gate'. Yet, in Kosovo, Bosnia, and even in Iraq, it is the Islamic element which is favored by the New World Order elite." Bis laughed, thinking, *"The Serbs were only fighting the Albanians*

for their historic land, willed to them by their ancestors, and to retain their orthodox Christian religion. One cannot just set aside such legitimate and historic based cultures, and traditions, of a people.

"*I remember the writings of a Kosovo Serb, who vividly described the never ending conflict between the West's Christianity, and the Middle East's Islam, saying, 'In the ebb and flow tides of this struggle, beginning in the Eighth Century, and continuing to the Twentieth Century, each side had two major advances, and two major reverses, approximately four centuries apart. We are now witnessing the fifth cycle, which is, for the first time, simultaneous. The West has been moving into the East economically and militarily. The Islamic tide, almost invisibly is seeping into the West, not by arms or economic power, but via steady immigration, settlements, threat of or actual violence, and ongoing demographic expansion.'*

"*That quote captures the truth perfectly,*" Bis continued thinking. "*The West will not survive if it depends on the New World Order, which is reliant on global institutions backed up by military power. The contest basically is that of ideas, traditions, and beliefs. It comes down to Christianity verses Islam.*"

Bis, pulling himself up to a standing position, began his walk back to the barracks, thinking, "*The 7th Stryker Regiment, and our own 7th Squadron, cannot really count on going home early from Iraq. In fact, I hope our tour is not extended. Bush and his neo-con handlers know their time is running out to reach a deal, while Bush is still president. But Bush knows, and Maliki knows, that some type of agreement must* be had, if the neo-cons intend to keep American troops in Iraq. Its UN Mandate expires December 31st.

"Maliki," Bis continued his thoughts, "*has the political advantage and he knows it. While he can talk about progress being determined by his government assuming control of the Iraqi provinces, his control is only tentative; one day he might, the next day he does not.*"

Bis laughed, "*Depends if his troops decide to back him, on that particular day, or if the threats or propositions of the Sunnis, or the Sadrists, look more dangerous, or more attractive.*"

Bis paled, however, thinking, "*What is really happening is Maliki is able to maneuver the agreement to where it is Maliki who actually controls when and where the US troops go. Maliki has the best of both worlds. While he cannot control his own military, and so, he must continue to have US protection, it is he who decides the fate of our GI's, keeping our American troops on his short leash. Not only that, but also insisting on the legal right for Iraqi judges to prosecute American soldiers at will for violating speculative Iraqi law.*

"*He has Bush by the gonads,*" Bis laughed, but cut his mirth short, realizing, "*Our sorry misbegotten adventure in Iraq to democratize the Islamic Middle East to salve our neo-con friends, and on behalf of our Maliki Arab Islamic friends, has put America on a strategic lifeline.*

"*All these six years in Iraq have been for naught,*" Bis pondered, intoning, "*As the French writer, LaFontaine told us, 'Nothing is more dangerous than a friend without discretion; even a prudent enemy is preferable.'"*

CHAPTER XX –
ISLAMIC TOLERANCE

Sunday, August 3, 2008, Bis, looking for a good nap, returned back to his barrack's after attending a Green Zone chapel service earlier, and then partaking in a generous breakfast with Corporal Tooley at the NCO Mess.

Bis did not attend church on every Sunday, but he always made sure he did when a particularly grizzled old Chaplain preached. Bis did not know his age, but he knew that this particular preacher had almost twenty years service in the Army Chaplain Corps. And yet was only a Captain. Bis also knew that this highly competent graduate of a well known Lutheran Seminary was kept at a lower rank because he insisted on invoking the name of Jesus Christ, after each prayer, and after each New Testament biblical admonition. This is a no-no in the current chaplain way of thinking. It is alright to use the word, "God", as it also can refer to the Jewish God, or the Islamic

Allah, but to say Jesus Christ, is to refer to Christianity, and that is, somehow, prejudicial, and therefore, not helpful to current religious diversity.

The Chaplain had not disappointed Bis. Bis laughed as he remembered listening to his sermon blasting his detractors, quoting, *"I Corinthians 6:9-10, 'Do you not know that the unrighteous will not inherit the Kingdom of God? Do not be deceived. Neither fornicators, nor idolaters, nor adulterers, nor homosexuals, nor sodomites, not thieves, nor coveters, nor drunkards, nor revilers, nor extortioners will inherit the Kingdom of God.' His acidly reminding the 'Chaplain powers that be', also that America still consists of a populace that is eighty percent strong Christian, with only one percent Muslim, and only two percent Jewish.*

"He rattled many Chaplains who are Rabbis, and who are now exerting more and more control in the Corps," Bis recalled. *"His Chaplain vividly pointed out, in his sermon, to anyone who would listen, that God's Ten Commandments were levied upon what were called Hebrews, not the Talmudic Jews. They not being in existence until twelve hundred years after the time of Abraham. He pointed out, original Hebrews came to be called Israelites, and the word Jews, which evolved much later, came from the Tribe of Judah, which actually formed only a one-twelfth part of the then Israel. The name Jesus was, at the time, derived from the small number of returnees to Jerusalem from their longtime Babylonian slavery. Bis' Chaplain also preached that Moses could not have been Jewish, as that word did not actually exist until several centuries after Moses' death.*

"*Thus my favorite Chaplain,*" Bis intoned, "*will remain only a Captain, until he retires, which I'm sure the rest of the Corps will hasten as much as possible. But it is more important to him, as it is to me, that Christianity must be described by referring to Jesus Christ and it is not to be used as a diversity. The molly-coddling of Rabbis or of Emirs, by misdirecting the use of Christ, either for some political purpose, or to gain the favor of Israel, or Maliki, cannot be condoned. Christianity must be preserved for Christians in the Middle East. It cannot be bartered away, or compromised, only to implement some agreement.*

"*Some way must be found, and quickly, to rescue this forced drowning of the very core of Christianity, the requirement that the Corps forbid the utterance of the very name Jesus Christ.*" Bis continued thinking, "*That such a thing could even occur is unbelievable. If such a thing had been tried in another era, or among the Americans founders, it would have been the fire producing another vigorous revolution.*"

Bis then clearly recalled, in his extensive reading of American history, how deeply Christian the founders really were, although many now try to find anti-Christian kinks in America's past. "*Accusing George Washington of deism is both a way of destroying Christianity, and at the same time, globalizing, and commercializing America.*"

Bis remembered reading a letter George Washington wrote in 1790, to a Hebrew congregation in Newport, Rhode Island, in a time frame during the adoption of the Constitution, but before the First Amendment, dealing with religious freedom, had been ratified. His letter reminded the Jews that, *"'America's religious toleration was not an indulgence for the lucky or the connected, but a natural right that patriots had died for, and is not to be confused with trying to bar freedom of continued religious expression by public officials.'"*

Bis also remembered his American History revealed Washington, after a military success in 1776, told his rag-tag army, *"'The blessing of Heaven and the bravery of our men, is only what can save America.'"* Chuckling, Bis then recalled, *"It was Washington who first endorsed paid chaplains for the troops. Is that not ironic to the attitude of the present day Corps."* Bis then concluded, *"Washington never questioned the relevance of Christianity as being indispensable to the moral, discipline, and good conduct of the men under his command.*

"But enough of this deep thinking," Bis said to himself, and he let out a big burst of stale air from his lungs, *"Now is a good time for a nap."*

It was not to be, as, just as Bis was somewhat settled in his un-cozy army cot, Tooley came barging in, obviously in a bad mood. He, with gusto, declared he had had a couple of beers at the NCO Club, and got engaged in a heated argument with a couple of unique Staff Sergeants, all of which led to their atheistic denial of the existence of Christ, himself. Not only that, but they also contended that Islam, historically, was more tolerant of its subjects than Christianity.

Tooley, laughing, interposed, "Rather than get in a fist fight with the bastards, I thought I would get some rebuttal information from my learned 7th

Squadron First Sergeant to throw at the unbelievers," adding, "I couldn't believe it, at first, that a couple of American sergeants would not spout Christianity first, last, and always, but these guys, before we got into the oral altercation, told me they were in Iraq, only on temporary assignment. They are part of the staff of Undersecretary of State, by the name of Karen Hughes, who is promoting an American Moslem group called the Islamic Society of North America, and are only in Iraq to advise the Bush people, who are trying to get an agreement with Maliki, to extend the American Forces Pact."

Bis, now thoroughly awake, pushed himself out of the cot, and sitting on its edge, pointed out to Tooley, "Hughes is a longtime advisor to Bush. He gave her the prestigious Department of State post to enable her to reach out to what Bush considers so-called moderate Moslems. This is, supposedly, Bush's underlying theme in Iraq, and elsewhere. He thinks we can find lots of moderate Islamists and reach out to their welcoming, outstretched arms, to form Bush's pro-Israel, pro-Western democracies."

Bis continued, "This is utter fantasy. You and I know that individual Moslem's lives are completely under the domination and control of the various Emirs. There is no such thing as a moderate Moslem. The current policy of a directing Emir could order mayhem or murder. Bush and his helpers never seem to grasp this fact," adding, "For instance, Hughes' underlying group, the Islamic Society of North America, which the staff sergeants are associated with, is completely financed and directed by Saudi Arabia. It preaches in Iraq and in America, the virtue of militant, anti-Christian, and anti-American Wahhabism, and always has. Why Hughes and Bush think they are a moderate Islamic group American can deal with, is stupidity. I think Bush and Hughes have been sipping some of that high point beer, my corporal found so appealing at the NCO Club," adding, "But the few American sergeants who profess atheism, or claim to have a tolerance for Islam, are just the kind of staffers Karen Hughes and Bush would want working with this advisory committee in Iraq."

"No lectures. Just give me some comeback pointers," laughed Tooley, "So I can get back to that high point beer at the club, and put down those liberal staffers."

Bis stood, walked to a window, gazed out of it for a few minutes, and then told Tooley, "When someone questions the existence of Christ, the best response I've found to that absurd assertion is one given by a writer by the name of Joe Sobran, who wrote of Christ, 'Can he be serious? The most famous and influential man who ever lived, never lived.

"'Can anyone really suppose such a marvelous character was invented? That a few unschooled and inartistic writers could have thought up immortal words suitable to him. That countless martyrs would endure agonizing death to bear witness to one whose reality was in doubt?'"

"That is really good," Tooley responded, writing down names and suggestions in a small notebook he started carrying in his shirt pocket.

"John Adams is another excellent quote," Bis continued, "He said, 'Christianity is a product of Devine revelation. Neither savage, nor civilized man, without a revelation, could ever have discovered it, or invented it.'"

Tooley nodded, and then disclosed, "Did you hear the latest? The Battalion First Sergeant told me that only a few days ago, Maliki deployed some of his best Iraqi troops, backed up by US helicopters, into the Sunni provincial government complex, in Baqouba, the Sunni Diyala provincial capital located about thirty-five miles northeast of Baghdad. He said they stormed the Sunni governor's office, killed his secretary, and four of his guards, and arrested the provincial security chief, accusing him of terrorism."

Bis responded, chuckling, "These prominent Sunni's had been hailed as the vanguard in forming a Sunni-Shi'ite, non-sectarian, all Iraq democratic government, by Bush adherents, just a few weeks ago," adding, "So much for Islamic tolerance, as your staff sergeants contend."

Bis continued, "Whether Bush believes it, or whether it is to further his total reliance on the neo-con-Israeli policies by contending there is such a thing as Islamic tolerance. The abetting media pundits keep emphasizing that, unlike historic Christians, Islamists have always allowed full religious freedom in their historical Muslim enclaves. That they were known for their so-called tolerance. This moral blindness, which underlies Bush's domestic American policy and also those in the Mid East, looking brainlessly for those mythical moderate Moslems to chair their committees, and fill their chaplain's seats, all aiming to develop their fairytale, everybody lives happily ever after, philosophy."

Tooley smiled, saying, "I hope you have some appropriate historical moments to enlighten me, non-sensing the so-called tolerance theme spouted by those two staff sergeants."

"What is the state religion in Egypt?" Bis unexpectedly asked.

"It is, of course, Islam," the Corporal replied. "It is a complete adherence, by Egypt's millions, to the edicts and Fatwa's of their Islamic Emirs."

Laughing, Bis disclosed, "Before the Egyptian nation was conquered by the heirs of Mohammad's militant Islam, in the eighth century, Egypt was almost one hundred percent Christian, a tribute to Christ's disciples."

"I don't believe it," Tooley replied, dumbfounded.

"It is true," Bis responded. "It is also true that for six hundred years after Egypt came under the domination of Islam, the Emirs did not insist on the destruction of Christianity, but they did not do it any favors. However, in the year 1345 AD, the flavor changed. While previously there had been periodic spasmodic persecution of Christians, it was mostly in and around Cairo. But the Fourteenth Century brought a new Emir driven intensity designed to ultimately destroy any Christian influence in Egypt. Mobs of Islamic terrorists instigated by the Emirs, forced innocent, cornered Christians to either recite the Muslim profession of faith, or they and their families, would be burned alive. Christian churches, and the estates of monasteries, were confiscated or destroyed, not only in Cairo, but throughout every village in Egypt. An Islamic favoring historian, al-Maqrizi, wrote at the time, 'Many Christian Copts converted to Islam, both in lower and upper Egypt. No church remained that had not been razed; on many of those sites, mosques were constructed - - - for when Christian afflictions grew great, and their incomes small, they decided to embrace Islam.'"

Bis continued, "Some modern historians have failed to truly describe this wrenching of Christianity out of the Egyptian people. They leave the impression, like Maqrizi that those changing cultures, came to acknowledge the superior virtues of Islam," adding, "Islamic persecution, when the Emirs did finally decide it was time, was extraordinarily savage and brutal, just like it is now in present day Iraq or in Saudi Arabia. Christians are without conscience murdered in bizarre evil ways. The aim today is the total elimination of Christianity in these nations."

Bis continued, "The Twelfth and Thirteenth Centuries marked further widespread Islam persecution and the destruction of Christianity in those lands that the Muslims had conquered in Asia and Africa. All the previous Christian states, that had existed on the African side of the Mediterranean Sea, were also forcibly converted, on penalty of death," adding, "It is astonishing to me how readily this myth of Muslim tolerance has been accepted. Those accustomed to a near total present day Muslim visible domination of all these nations comprising the Middle East, it would probably be incredible for them to imagine that a different situation had ever existed, particularly that these same nations had, at one time, a majority Christian background. That those historic facts not known, however, can be explained, and blamed on the failure of our leaders and teachers to become aware of these facts, as they should be."

Bis concluded, "As it was aptly described by one writer, 'The deeply rooted Christianity of Africa and Asia did not simply fade away. It was crushed.' And that conclusion would also include early Israel, the entire early Middle East, and much of the Far East. If the world fails to understand that Islam is, in fact, the Lucifer led satanic enemy of Christianity, then it does not truly understand what history tells us. They continue pursuing an unreachable fairytale."

Tooley breathed out the involuntary air held in his lungs, and sadly pointed out, "Christianity, it seems, is being attacked on all sides. A few days ago, an Alabama judge was reported to have been cited by a judicial inquiry commission as violating his judicial ethics, by merely holding hands in his court, and praying, telling people in his courtroom that he was not afraid to call out the name, Jesus," adding, "Those who should be defending Christianity are badly fumbling their jobs. They are preaching, in essence, that the truths of Christianity are profane, while their profound atheistic illusions of doctored up Christianity, is sacred."

Bis nodded in agreement, pointing out, "The Vatican reluctantly admitted, a few weeks ago, that for the first time in history, Islam has surpassed Catholics in numbers in the world, by nineteen point percent to seventeen point four percent. Muslims make lots of children, was the explanation."

"We Christians all have an enormous job to do," Tooley responded, patting Bis on the back as he prepared to leave, and declaring in his lingering, beer inspired, louder than usual voice, "Thanks to you, my good sergeant, I now have the ammunition I need to bury those corrupt, greedy, perfidious, fanatic, bigoted, fraudulent, atheistic staff sergeants, in a rattlesnake pit of high point beer.

"I shall not fail you," he exclaimed, laughing. "I shall do my duty to the last drop."

Chapter XXI – "Under Maliki Command"

Late in the day on August 5, 2008, a staff corporal wandered into the 7th Stryker Squad's barracks, looking for a Sergeant Bismarck.

He was quickly led to Bis' semi-private enclave, where he informed the Sergeant, "What I have to say is confidential."

Bis, laughing, told the squadsman to scat, and was then informed by the messenger that the Major wanted to see him at 10:00 a.m., in his office, the following day, for sure, emphasizing "for sure".

Knowing that there were a thousand reasons the Major would want to see him, good or bad, Bis quickly gave up on speculating why.

It was, however, with a sense of anxiety, that Bis was ushered into the Major's, now familiar, office, at the appointed time.

As he saluted, Bis said, "You wanted to see me, sir."

"The Silver Star," the Major responded. "I have highly recommended you to the 711th Stryker Brigade commander to be a proper recipient of the prestigious Silver Star medal, and I also suggested that the commander present it to you in front of the entire brigade."

Bis smiled at the offer, replying, "Any Stryker in the brigade would be proud and humble."

"I'm not sure anyone else but you would be so humble," the Major interposed, adding, "The Star language, governing its award, calls for gallantry in action, and I have seen very few, other than you, who fill that bill.

"Oh, by the way," the Major continued, "the Captain was not so recommended. Its not that he wasn't brave and gallant, just what happened in Rashad and in his rescue, was your show."

Bis nodded, but made no comment, knowing there had to more of a reason for this get-together.

Clearing his throat, the Major then commented, "After I had submitted my recommendations to Brigade, I was called by an officer on the Brigade Commander's staff. He told me that the staff was concerned about Sergeant Bismarck's free wheeling comments concerning General Petraeus, President Bush, and other Washington officials about the conduct of this Iraq deployment."

Bis paled at this disclosure, but said nothing.

"I know you value your independent opinions and thoughts highly," the Major continued. "I am hoping you can be a little more discrete with your comments until we get this medal thing over."

"I would rather have my independent opinions," Bis responded, "than the Silver Star."

Taken aback by this admission, the Major then intoned, "I was sure, in my heart, that you probably would say it just like you did," adding, "Sometimes, however, discretion is the better part of valor."

"The whole Iraq misadventure," Bis interposed, "including America's initial Iraqi invasion, is a result of replacing valor with something else. The results are five thousand GI's dead, the American military shattered, and three trillion dollars in debt."

Bis continued, "It proves the old saying, "What goes around, comes around. In March of 2003, Saddam Hussein, and his Sunni government, represented a valid check on the Shi'ites in Iraq, and also on the Iranian Shi'ites. Bush and his neo-cons conspired to bring Saddam to defeat, through blatant lies to the American people, and thus, destroyed those crucial, vital checks. The intervening five years of war in Iraq has centered mainly on trying to restore those vital checks," adding, "A few weeks ago, through prodding, by Petraeus and Bush, the Maliki Shi'ite Iraqi government, agreed to fill six long time vacant seats in his Cabinet with six Sunnis from the Sunni Parliament Bloc, "The National Accordance Front", which group had boycotted the government for a year. Bush continues to pressure Maliki to work toward a so-called reconciliation of Iraqi Sunni, and Shi'ite, as Bush's continuing recipe for his democratizing of Iraq. Sunnis, who represent twenty percent of Iraq, were actually the new force behind Bush's surge. They did so through being bribed with tons of American money, and by the re-establishing of anti-al-Qaeda "Awakening Councils", not love of Bush."

Bis continued, "A few days ago, in the Sunni run and occupied Anbar Province, General Kelly, commander of the thirty-seven thousand mostly Marines, who have bravely fought many historic battles against the Sunnis in the past, was evidently ordered by the Petraeus command, to make a big show of turning over that Sunni Province, the cradle of the previous Sunni insurgency, to our new, bribed, Sunni allies, the new awakened Iraqi troops."

The Major interrupted, saying, "You are aware that the turning over ceremony was held under the utmost security, and in the easily protected center of Ramadi, the capital of Anbar. Kelly's Marines also provided the sole security."

"Prime Minister Nouri al-Maliki noticeably snubbed the ceremony," Bis responded. "The Anbar Sunnis also publicly criticized the Maliki government for failing to embrace the turnover. The Sunni-Shi'ite war, feud, and fuss is painfully still evident. Bush and Petraeus are brainlessly counting on a continued Sunni surge support for their policy, but that support will last only so long as they continue to pay the bribes to the Sunni chiefs and Emirs with many US dollars. When that stops, or wanes, the supporting will stop. Anbar is now, however, unfortunately, back in Sunni hands. Petraeus contends the Sunni Anbars will take the lead in security, but General Kelly cautions correctly that Anbar will remain secure only because of his twenty-five thousand Marines, which still remain in control of Anbar, providing military control.

"Kelly also lost eight helicopters, including the CH-53 Sea Stallions, and four Cobras, along with several Marine detachments, which have been ordered to Afghanistan," the Major intoned.

"Bush and Petraeus still have overwhelming problems trying to coalition the Iraqi Sunnis, and Maliki," Bis pointed out. "The Iraqi government consistently has strongly resisted incorporating Sunni troops into the Iraqi Security Forces. My information is that a pitiful few six hundred Sunnis, more or less, out of a supposed one hundred three thousand Iraqi troops are currently active in the Security Force. The Pentagon, however, is continuing to push hard to include more Sunni, or 'Sons of Iraq', as they call themselves, but Maliki is throwing up-road blocks wherever he can, calling the Sunnis hooligans."

"Maliki reportedly has instructed his Shi'ite Security Force to arrest or kill any Sunni group leaders whenever they can," the Major disclosed.

"That does not make for a unified command," Bis chuckled, adding, "The Sons of Iraq could easily restart back fighting Shi'ites, and then use that as an excuse to killing GI's, especially when Maliki is only willing to give the Sunnis the most low level jobs like what they call the 'enlisted beat cop', which is down as low on the Iraqi social scale as you can get."

The Major nodded, and commented, "Bush is also trumpeting what he calls a breakthrough in reaching an agreement to extend the 'Status of Forces' agreement, but rather than a formal compact, Maliki is describing it as a 'Memorandum of Understanding' (MOU)."

"A Memorandum of Understanding is, at the most, only an expression of good will," Bis offered. "It is not an enforceable contract, or an obligation of resources. It means nothing," adding, "If it is imposed, I would be terrified to allow my Squadron to do anything, because the Maliki government, able to prosecute anything, could assume legal jurisdiction over any of my troops' actions, after the December 31st UN Mandate expires."

"That's true," admitted the Major. "Several American legal scholars have unequivocally stated that an MOU does not have any particular legal force, especially when it has not been ratified by the Iraqi Parliament."

"It is unbelievable to watch Bush accepting such half measures," interpled Bis. "It is proof to me that he and his neo-cons are losing their control in Iraq and the whole situation could burst wide open."

"Bush and Maliki, in deference, are pushing for the establishment of a Joint Committee, consisting of Americans and Iraqis, to resolve each issue as it comes up," the Major pointed out. "This could easily end up subjecting our GI's to being unjustly prosecuted in corrupt Iraqi courts, rather than under the usual American Court Martial Code."

"It would, for sure, put Americans under the jurisdiction of a Moslem foreign culture, including a set of Emir created, non-descript laws, which have no American constitutional protections," Bis asserted. "Yet American GI's must go where they are ordered to go, or be labeled criminals," adding, "Bush, however, and his neo-cons, along with the whole liberal bunch in Congress, and also in the opinion of at least four members of the current Supreme Court, would actively promote such a legal state of affairs. None of them would seriously object to it."

"Just who are Americans anymore?" the Major questioned. "Do we really have a persona anymore? Does it make any difference?"

"There is still a big, vital difference between Native Americans, and the rest of the world," Bis intoned. "Although America is involuntarily hosting twenty million illegal, Hispanics, who are definitely not Americans."

Bis continued, "The historic Americans, who, for the most part, are descended from immigrating Europeans over the course of three hundred years. It is the unique composition of the North American continent that developed those certain identifiable traits and behaviors which make us Americans. If it had not been for the abundance of space and land, which we lump together, over the course of years, as the frontier, America would have merely digressed into just another stratified, socialized, upper class-lower class, European state."

"What do you mean?" asked the Major.

"From our beginnings, up to the 1890's, America was shaped by its wild, wild West," Bis responded. "Germans, Irishmen, Englishmen, Swedes, and others, came to America looking for a new life. What they found, highly different from Europe, was land. Landless peasants in Europe became landowners in America. By perspiration and self-reliance, they prospered with this abundant land beyond their wildest expectations, not only during one generation, but over several generations, stretching for two hundred years. Germans, Irish, English, and Swedes remained, figuratively, as Germans, Irish, English, and Swedes, but they also were ground into a different nationality. They became real, true blooded, certified Americans. The West not only shaped them with its abundance of land, but it also offered them other vocations, and avocations, such as metals, timber, coal, iron, and cattle land grazing. As has been historically pointed out, the frontier reinforced and exaggerated the American traits and built its unique characteristics."

"If you add in the fact that many frontier Americans also moved freely and did so several times, engaging in several occupations, also militating against a ridged class system," suggested the Major.

Bis nodded in agreement, saying, "From working the farms, to cutting timber, trapping furs, and panning for gold, these opportunities created self-reliant individuals," adding, "As an example, an Irish immigrant by the name of King, came to Texas as a twelve-year-old stow-away. He ended up owning and operating a one million acre land conglomerate, which became known as the King Ranch. Another fifteen-year-old, named Longbaugh, headed west from Pennsylvania, becoming infamously known as the 'Sundance Kid'."

Bis continued, "Most Americans living out on our frontiers, more especially people living as mountain men, sourdoughs, cowboys, teamsters, and other rugged types, judged men solely on their talents, and their survival merits, not on the titles, or the money, which happened to be in their pockets.

"Thus, when a titled Englishman demanded that an American cowboy he had hired, fill a bathtub brought West for the occasion, the cowboy drew his six-gun and shot the bathtub full of holes, saying," Bis chuckled, "'Now you have a shower,' or another, 'That you may be a Lord, back in England, but that ain't what you are out here.'"

The Major laughed out loud, commenting, "Just about all of our families, such as mine, who settled in the Middle West, could tell similar tales."

"A bigger modern problem," Bis commented, "is not only the obvious illegal Hispanic invasion of America, who never the less claim citizenship privileges, while denouncing the usual American traits, but also the phenomenon known as 'anchor babies', and another called dual citizenship. Both are rapidly bringing down sovereign America, even as they claim American rights."

Bis continued, "Five hundred thousand babies are born each year in America whose mothers are illegals. That amounts to ten percent of all births. These babies are given automatic American citizenship, under a tortured interpretation of the Fourteenth Amendment, which grants the same to American births, but also qualifies this precious right by demanding that such birth be subject to the jurisdiction of the US," adding, "The granting of illegal birthright is the product of our usual over-reaching federal judges."

The Major shook his head and murmured, "To get the Supreme Court to change would be daunting to say the least."

"If the Congress were lucid, they might understand that the Constitution gives sole citizenship and naturalization authority to Congress," Bis pointed out, adding, "All the salons have to do is pass a law which relates, if a child is born to an illegal alien in the US, that child is not a citizen. That's it. The end."

"The biggest game in town, and in America," the Major contended, "is who can fool the American people the most, and the longest."

"Another seemingly simple job for the Congress is to eliminate dual citizenship," Bis intoned. "Right now, even if a Mexican obtains citizenship through naturalization, and becomes a bona fide American citizen, Mexico allows him to also keep his Mexican citizenship, and to vote in Mexican elections. The citizenship oath is clear enough. He must renounce all allegiance to any foreign prince, potentate, state, or sovereignty, and Congress can easily legislate a mandate to revoke their American citizenship if they do so."

Bis stood, and told the Major, "I will not manufacture my opinions and thoughts to conform to what Bush and Petraeus thinks is proper. If I did, I would be living and fomenting a lie. A lie that would compromise my very soul," adding, "Not only is it wrong, but as my ancient friend, Aristotle, once said, 'Liars, having spun spurious facts for even a brief moment, when they then start speaking the truth, are not believed.' I would rather be believed first, last and always."

The Major smiled and then intoned, "You are, of course, right. Looking at it from a practical viewpoint, I don't think its necessary. Brigade, would risk a revolt, like they have never seen before, if they turn down this Silver Star."

CHAPTER XXII – SUNNI VS. SHI'ITE REMATCH

The dog days of August, both in America, and in Iraq, crawled along at a snail's pace. Bis and his Squadron spent most of their time looking for things to do in the Green Zone. Fortunately, the Strykers had not been called upon to deploy into any combat situation. Some of the Squadsmen complained they would rather, rather than sit around in the heat.

Tooley and Bis celebrated the welcomed Labor Day holiday, drinking beer in the NCO Club, and toasting anyone and everyone whose name had anything to do with American labor. It was, however, mostly an exercise in flexing the imbibing elbow.

"I do have a lot of respect for the average American working guy," Bis told the Corporal, "Union or non-union," adding, "Not the union hierarchy. They are only parasites, but the vast majority of the working stiffs. They, for the most part, are excellent, hardworking, knowledgeable, highly proficient, and loyal Americans, and also mostly practicing Christians."

Bis continued, "We do, however, have to toast Peter J. McGuire, the secretary of the 'Brotherhood of Carpenters and Joiners', who founded the 'American Federation of Labor'. It was he, in 1882, who suggested the original 'Workman's Holiday', honoring those, 'who from rude nature have delved and carved all the grandeur we behold.'"

Tooley, gazing at Bis in amazement at the ever ready fountain of information, raised his glass of beer in a toast, and then said, "I suppose we should also toast the just completed Democrat and Republican conventions."

Bis smiled, and then, in an elaborate right arm motion, poured out the remainder of his glass in a nearby bowl, and turned his glass upside down on the table.

Tooley laughed, and then, changing the subject, told Bis, "The Brigade First Sergeant announced that Bush and company have authorized a couple of thousand Marines to move out of Iraq, hopefully to go back to their American bases. They have also authorized sending a couple of other Marine units from Iraq to Afghanistan."

Bis nodded, "One of the Iraqi Brigades is also going to be deployed to Afghanistan. That would reduce the Brigade numbers to fourteen in Iraq."

"That's a loss of four to five thousand troops in Iraq," Tooley calculated, adding, "There will also probably be more troops pulled out of Iraq and put into Afghanistan soon, if the Taliban's unexpectedly strong uprising continues. US forces are too few, and NATO forces are next to worthless."

"Bush also talks about bringing two Brigades home, which amounts to eight thousand men, soon," Bis claimed. "The question is how soon? There are no more available American troops, either in Iraq or in America. No matter how bad it looks, it is going to get worse."

"If there are one hundred forty thousand troops now in Iraq," Tooley continued, still calculating, "and if troops are reduced in Iraq by even only the small numbers we are talking about, that would leave, at the most, one hundred twenty-five thousand GI's."

"It could be a whole lot more going from Iraq, if there are significantly new attacks on our troops in Afghanistan, resulting in significant loss of American lives," Bis countered.

"Do you think the 711th Brigade has a chance to be one of the Brigades that is given a ticket back to the good, old USA?" asked Tooley.

"Not a chance in a million," Bis responded, laughing. "Although if my Bush-Petraeus remarks keep getting reported to the staff at Brigade, they might send me home."

"What's that?" asked Tooley. "I don't think any of the 7th Squadron would be a rat. Probably one of them might have repeated a remark or two of yours to someone in the 3rd Squadron. I'll tell them to be careful."

"Don't do that," cautioned Bis. "I don't want to accuse anyone, and I certainly don't want to cover up anything I said."

Bis abruptly got up, bringing back two bottles of American beer from the NCO bar, and, as he placed one bottle before the Corporal, commented, "I am more than anything else, deeply concerned about the continued, and continuing instability in Iraq, particularly, since Bush and his neo-cons are being forced to rob Iraq's Peter to pay Afghanistan's Paul, to cover Bush's withdrawal mistakes there. Bush has granted Maliki, and his corrupt Shi'ite government, too much leeway. I'm also concerned that Bush is willing, trying to claim victory, to turn over to our former Sunni enemies, the huge and strategic province of Anbar. It would not take much to make Hussein's Sunnis our enemies again. Just a word from one of their Emir-chiefs would probably do it."

"You are right," Tooley replied, taking a sip of his new beer. "It is big. It stretches all the way from just east of Baghdad to the borders of Syria, Jordan, and Saudi Arabia."

"It also controls all the main roads into Jordan and Syria," Bis intoned.

"The elaborate turnover ceremonies done in secret, and guarded by US Marines, in the more secure center of Ramadi, does not speak too highly of being able to depend on Sunni security forces to be on board Maliki's government," Tooley also offered.

In fact, a Sunni spokesman criticized the Maliki Shi'ites for their failure to attend and embrace the turnover ceremonies," Bis interposed, emphasizing the true fact that the Sunni-Shi'ite continuing war is just below the surface."

Bis continued, "If you also consider, seriously, the previous turnovers of Dhiqar, Muthanna, Wasit, Babel, and Qadislyah Provinces in the Shi'ite south, all leading to the port city of Basra, and all of which are no longer guarded by the long gone British troops. Whether the provinces might be controlled by Maliki, is iffy. They also could each be controlled by Sadr's Shi'ite forces," adding, "But the big problem is that all the main roads from Baghdad south to Basra, including the Iraq super-highways along the Tigris River, and the other Iraq super-highways along the Euphrates River, which is now the American's only means of getting vital supplies to the troops, is fully dependent on so-called Shi'ite security troops."

"Who they are loyal to is a good question," Tooley agreed, taking another swig of beer. "As a matter of fact, they seem to switch allegiance back and forth, depending on who is talking to them at the time."

"This south Shi'ite area, which historically includes the ruins of Ur," the ancient capital of the Sumerian civilization, and the biblical home of the prophet Abraham, is also the home of several active, presumptively Sadr, militias."

Tooley grinned, saying, "You had to throw that Abraham thing in, didn't you?"

Bis, chuckling out loud, then stated, "Basra, with its seat on the Persian Gulf and nearness to Kuwait, would, if a problem arose, be the only means by which the US could be able to evacuate, both its valuable and extensive, expensive, crucial equipment, such as our million dollar each, eight wheel, all wheel drive, armored Strykers, along with our valuable Squadsmen, such as the distinguished Corporal Tooley, of the 7th Squadron."

"Okay, I'll quit trying to be funny, if you quit trying to be funny," Tooley urged, smiling, adding, "The apparent problems, however, are not funny," as he took a long drink of beer.

"Just look at the recent turmoil going on in Iraq, and in only the past few months," Bis cautioned. "This is the period which Bush and Petraeus portray as the so-called time of victory achieved by their non-existent surge. In Diyala Province, for instance, a few miles west of Baghdad, only three weeks ago, a suicide bomber blew herself up in a group of Sunni 'Awakening Council' security troops, which included some US troops, in Baqouba, killing thirty Sunni and five GI's. This supposedly was an area which should have remained cleaned completely out of Sadr sympathizers. Remember our several trips into Baqouba?"

Tooley nodded.

"Evidently we didn't get them all. They still seem to be a potent, every ready, force," admitted Bis.

"And look at the suburb of Baghdad, called Azamiyah, where the 7th had a big fight with Sadr Shi'ites. This is in the area where the US built the obnoxious defensive concrete wall," Bis maintained. "This suburb was one of the chief Saddam Hussein, Sunni, former resistance spots. It is now the site of one of the main, so-called Sunni Awakening Councils," adding, "Just a few days ago, a Shi'ite woman suicide bomber detonated herself in the middle of this Awakening Council, killing the Sunni leader and several of his Sunni security guards. This atrocity could be attributed to either Sadr or to Maliki. Either way, it points out that the current Iraqi situation remains highly volatile and unstable."

"Its not just Shi'ite attacking Sunni," Tooley added, "Just south of Baghdad, in the Shi'ite city of Karbala, last week, several suicide bombers attacked Shi'ite Islamic pilgrims, who by the thousands, had gathered in that city. The terrorists were obviously Sunnis who wanted retribution for earlier Shi'ite attacks on Sunnis."

He continued, "Several Shi'ites were killed outright, with scores wounded."

Bis nodded, "I think that some of the Sunni Emirs intentionally ordered that attack, trying to re-ignite the Sunni-Shi'ite wars," adding, "They see less and less of an American Iraqi presence, and are determined to break off a part of Iraq for the Sunnis," adding, "Just two days ago, in the usually peaceful Shi'ite city of Dujail, which is about fifty miles north of Baghdad, a car bomb detonated in front of the Shi'ite police station, killing thirty-five Shi'ites, including ten Shi'ite policemen."

"That's getting close to the Kurd's Territory, including their main cities of Mosul and Kirkuk," Tooley intoned. "While Kurds are sometimes labeled Sunnis, they are really a religion of their own, and I doubt whether they instigated the, obviously, coordinated attack."

Bis nodded in agreement, and taking the last drink of his beer, commented, "You are right. The attack had to be put together by the Anbar Sunnis.

The Sunni Emirs probably hoped that the Kurds and the Shi'ites would start fighting again."

Bis continued, "As far as I'm concerned, the Kurds, who don't seem to have big objections to Christian Iraqis, including the conversion to Christianity of some of their own Kurds, have no need to fight. They already have the best of both worlds. They enjoy complete autonomy from Maliki's so-called Iraqi government, while at the same time, holding sufficient seats in the parliament, the key to keeping Maliki in the majority. They, in short, have Maliki by the gonads. If push comes to shove, that's where I'm heading. There would be a reasonable likelihood that American troops would not be attacked by Kurds," adding, "Also, the city of Mosul is the home of the historical remnants of the main cities of the ancient Assyrian Empire, Nineveh and Nimrud."

"There you go again with that ancient stuff," Tooley chided, "but I agree, the Kurds, with their own army, and with their own lucrative oil wells, are more or less on their own sovereign ground," adding, "They have already made deals with various oil companies, along with contracting with Red China."

"You can see what China thinks about the happenings in Iraq," laughed Bis, adding, "You can also draw your own conclusions about the Iraqi situation, by watching the happenings in Anbar. Whiles Bush lauds the turnover of the province to America's former bitter Sunni enemies, Maliki has ordered his Shi'ite Iraqi security troops to kill and arrest these latter day Awakening Council Sunnis. It is the Maliki order that will control," adding, "As has been pointed out, 'The real mistake is that from which we learn nothing.'"

"I like Yogi Berra's comment better," Tooley intoned, "'If you don't know where you are going, you might wind up someplace else.'"

Bis laughing, murmured, "Take note Mr. Bush. Take note."

Chapter XXIII – The Star

The first two weeks of September, 2008, evidenced with Bis a continued proof that fatal US troop incidents in Afghanistan were increasing, with Pakistan also exhibiting a tendency to being a very reluctant ally.

Afghan insurgents, in that time frame, mounted two of their biggest attacks on American and Western military forces in several years. A score of French soldiers had been killed, and many were wounded in a mountain ambush. This attack, in addition, was a frontal attack, highly unusual for the Taliban, and was estimated to number over one hundred terrorists. The successful attack was also carried out only thirty miles east of Kabul, the Afghanistan capital.

Another troubling set of facts, which deeply disturbed Bis, was when he learned of the audacious terrorist frontal attack on US forces in Afghanistan, and only one thousand yards from the GI's base entrance. *"Though US fighter planes were quickly called in, there were still several GI's killed by the terrorist's unremitting attacks,"* adding, *"Increased Taliban activity will probably cause France to cancel its agreement to send seven hundred more troops to Afghanistan,"* Bis thought. *"So few, but every bit helps to keep my Brigade out of Afghanistan."*

On Thursday, 9-11-08, the anniversary of the New York Islam tower attacks, the Major sent word to Bis that both had withstood the verbal attacks on Bis by the Brigade staff, which wanted to cancel the awarding of the Silver Star, because of alleged hostile remarks made about Bush-Petraeus actions in Iraq. The Major's message conveyed that the Brigade Commander was well aware of the huge disruption that would arise out of the ranks, if the medal was not presented. Also, another saving grace for the medal pinning, was the fact that General David Petraeus was being kicked upstairs, and would no longer be the commanding general in Iraq. This job was being given to a Petraeus clone, a General Raymond Odierno, and the turnover ceremony was for the sixteenth of September. This caused the Brigade CO to wisely arrange the "Star" award pinning date to be September 17th, a time before any brass above would be able to stop it. The announcement of the award, the Major said, would be conveyed to all Brigade lesser commanders on September 15, 2008, with the ceremony scheduled to be in front of the assembled Brigade at 0900 hours, in the Green Zone parade ground. The Green Zone Marching Band has also been notified.

The Major closed his message, disclosing, *"I have been given the honor to escort you to the Brigade Commander, for the medal pinning. I am truly grateful for the task. So, my friend, be fully prepared for this assignment. You will be picked up at your barracks at 0700. Be ready."*

Bis, except for Tooley, kept this information to himself, and admonished the Corporal to do the same.

By the fifteenth, however, general notice of the award was being given throughout the Green Zone, and Bis was constantly congratulated by all who met him. The evening of the sixteenth, after chow at the NCO mess, Bis made his way back to his barracks intending on early to bed. As he sauntered through the barrack door, as the result of a well planned Tooley escapade, two of his squadsmen walked up to his front, while two others lingered behind. One of them then knelt down. The other three moved, and quickly pushed Bis backward into a prone position, after which all four then picked him up and carried the smiling Bis three times throughout the barracks, all to the discordant chorus of "He is a Jolly Good Fellow". They then dumped him, unceremoniously, on his cot. But all then stood solemnly, forming a congratulatory line, and individually honored and lauded Bis.

To Bis, this ceremony with his Squad was much more important than the coming, formal, medal pinning.

However, precisely at 0900 hours, on the seventeenth, Bis, who had earlier retrieved from the bottom of his foot locker, a seldom used uniform that had been especially tailored while Bis was stationed at Des Moines. It had been immaculately cleaned, starched, and pressed, showing its hardly used, bright First Sergeant stripes, and with its brass shining to a glow, made the ideal model of the perfect, six foot, well proportioned, American soldier, as Bis performed the precise military maneuvers, behind the Major, ending up in front of the scowling Brigade Commander. After an aide quickly read the Citation of Bravery, by Ian Otto von Bismarck, of Newtown, Iowa, the reluctant officer pinned the Silver Star on Bis' uniform chest. Bis then saluted and to the un-military cheers of the troops, made an about face. Bis, the Major, and the CO stood rigidly at attention, while the band played "*Stars and Stripes Forever*", and all the rest of the Brigade passed in review. Clearly, by the actions of the smiling GI's, it was a review they obviously relished.

The "Star" ceremony over, Bis thanked the Major, for all he had done. As he left, he told the Major he continued to worry about the ultimate safety of his Squadron. Declaring that though there were not presently fixed battles, there were the continuing obvious signs of unrest. Sunni and Shi'ite religious war was still ongoing, and a constant fight for turf prevailed. Maliki's government also continues to shut out the Sunnis and his security troops continue to kill and arrest Sunni Awakening Council officers with abandon, even though Bush and the US Iraqi High Command insist on their inclusion in the Shi'ite government. Bush's unsteady hand in controlling things in Iraq is getting more and more iffy in Bis' mind. The Major, as Bis departed, nodded in agreement with the assessment.

By the last of September, Bis was getting more nervous, as he saw troops leaving for home, and deploying to Afghanistan.

Bis noted that Sharia Law was also making itself felt on the world level. He was aware of the goings on of the United Nations' Human Rights Council, always known for its corruptness and its poor decisions. *"The makeup of the United Nations itself,"* Bis thought, *"was the Islamic states' increasing their numbers and their unity, and is clearly showing a Moslem balance of power running that organization. The Council now chaired by Cuba, protects Sharia Law, and at the same time, condemns any attack on Islamic's many worldwide human rights violations."*

Bis told Tooley, as they discussed these continuing, growing problems, during their daily treks to the NCO Mess, "Bush, in his eagerness to cow-tow and please Israel, and the neo-cons, has no conception of the harm he is doing to America in his new attacks on Russia. Calling Russian actions in Georgia, 'an affront to civilized standards,' was stupid. Without going into the merits of the Civil War, since prior to the war, the enclaves of Ossetia and Abkhazia, already considered themselves defacto Russian citizens. The thing that concerns me is, as a result, Russia has ended its cooperation with NATO. Because of Bush's tirades, he has put in jeopardy one of America's vital supply routes to our troops in Afghanistan. Since the installation of the new government of Asif Ali

Zardari in Pakistan, they have also halted, they say only temporarily, our other usual routes of bringing through material to Iraq. But supplying our troops could still be a big problem. Russian cooperation with America is vital in many of our ongoing operations. To brainlessly and clumsily berate Russia, like Bush is doing, is going to hurt America more than Russia."

Tooley, sipping his coffee, nodded in agreement, saying, "Just a few days ago, our so-called ally, Pakistan, authorized its military forces to open fire on US forces if they should launch any more raids into Pakistan, even going after Taliban terrorists, according to the First Sergeant," adding, "No Western country can really depend on any long term allegiance by any Islamic nation. Russia, is, after all, a Christian country, and should be basically aligned with Western interests. It would be a disaster to alienate them.

"Another interesting thing, the Brigade First Sergeant told me," Tooley commented, "is that General George Casey, who was General David Petraeus' predecessor from June of 2004 to February of 2007, in June 2007, was accosted by a General Jack Keane, a Bush troubleshooter, and a cloned Bush General, while Casey happened to be at Walter Reed Army Medical Center for a routine medical checkup. Keane told Casey, 'We feel – you are too out in front, advocating a policy for which you are not accountable,' to which Casey replied, 'We're accountable – you're not accountable, and that's a problem.' The First Sergeant also told me that at an August 2008 meeting at Dick Cheney's Washington residence, Keane told those present that General Petraeus had an unsupportive chain of command, which he claimed was the first time this happened in Petraeus' career, claiming that it had an adverse impact on Petraeus. Keane also complained to Cheney that Secretary Gates was not doing enough to enlist support in Congress for Petraeus, and for Ambassador Ryan Crocker. Keane complained that the Defense Department was 'more concerned about breaking the Army and Marine Corps, than winning the war!'"

"Thank God for that," Bis intoned, chuckling. "Where does your Brigade Sergeant get all his information?"

"He says he listens into the conversations his CO has with the ongoing gossip with the higher brass," Tooley replied. "Its like being briefed personally by the Pentagon," adding, "He also said that Admiral Bill Fallon, who was Chief of Central Command at the time, recommended to Gates that Petraeus be replaced, back in October of 2007, as he was buckling under a severe strain. Further, that the National Security Advisor, Steven Hadley was the big player in forcing Bush's ideas on everyone, and that it was Bush's instincts, rather than a deliberate policy making process that was in play."

"I would not doubt that at all," Bis admitted. "Did the Brigade Sergeant have any comment on the new Iraq commander, General Ray Odierno?"

"That is the new news for the coming week," laughed Tooley.

"I was more surprised by Petraeus' final comments at the turnover, rather than any assessment of Odierno, who, by all reports is merely another Bush clone," Bis admitted. "Petraeus said, 'The insurgents and militia extremists - - - are now weakened, but not yet fully defeated.' He then said, which I think is the more revealing, 'When I took the Iraq assignment in February 2007, the situation was hard but not hopeless.' After thanking the troops, Petraeus said, 'You have turned hard, but not hopeless into still hard but hopeful.' This can't be good news for Bush and the neo-cons, but to his credit, it is an admission of 'hard facts'. The stability situation in Iraq has not really improved, even after all Bush and America has invested."

Bis continued, "When you also consider the consequences of the, unlikely to occur, Japanese Prime Minister Fukuda's recent resignation, as also affecting my Squadron here in Iraq, in many ways, though half a world away, I get more jumpy."

Tooley looked at Bis with a puzzled frown. "What do you mean?"

"Japanese warships have for several years helped to refuel American and NATO cargo carriers, which are supplying American troops in both Iraq and in Afghanistan, during their trip through the Indian Ocean," Bis explained. "When the Prime Minister resigns, it means that the Japanese authority to continue that operation will have to be renewed in the Japanese 'diet'. It, now, unfortunately, will expire at the end of 2008, and renewal is no longer a sure thing."

"Things can really get complicated," Tooley interpled. "Things you really don't think about," adding, Like why does Bush, every year now, since

2000, give a state dinner honoring one hundred or so American Muslims at the White House, when each of these Islamic hypocrites hate Christians, hate Americans, and will do everything in their power to destroy America."

"The rank stupidity of our American political leadership, from the presidency through the Congress, and also on the high court, has been apparent for decades," Bis murmured. "It exemplifies one of Andrew Carnegie's observations to explain things. He is quoted as saying, 'As I grow older, I pay less attention to what men say. I just watch what they do.'"

Tooley could not suppress an expressed belly laugh, commenting, "Old Andrew was not burdened, or contaminated by the present university system brainwashing in citing that wisdom."

CHAPTER XXIV –
THE UNDER CURRENT

The Baghdad heat, actually and figuratively, continued into the middle of October, 2008.

Beyond that, Bis could feel a growing under current gripping the band-aid held together piece of earth, called Iraq. It was the same feeling that one gets, after lighting the fuse on a firecracker, but it does not go off when it's supposed to.

That changed, however, as on Sunday, October 11th, after weeks of non-deployment, the 7th Stryker Calvary Regiment, which included Bis' Squadron, of the 711th Stryker Brigade, suddenly received orders to move, posthaste to the Sunni city of Ramadi, located a few miles east of Baghdad. It is the main city in Iraq's Anbar Province, the recently turned over Sunni stronghold, to satisfy the Bush-Petraeus victory call. Sunni security troops were supposedly in charge, all part of the newly allied Sunni Awakening Councils. Somehow Shi'ite terrorists had avoided the supposed heavy Sunni guards, and a suicide blew up in the middle of a "Council" meeting, killing a dozen Sunni leaders, and injuring twenty bystanders. It was supposed to be the 7th Squadron's job to make sure things did not get out of control.

As Bis' Squadron moved toward Ramadi, which also formed a key part of the Iraqi highway network leading to Syria, Lebanon, and the Persian Gulf, he noticed, what appeared to be, unattached Sunnis with slung AK-47's, hanging out without reason, around the centers of the various villages on the way, including the big Sunni city of Fallujah. Bis got an eerie sensation watching them, knowing they could be a formidable force if the Awakening Council Emirs called them to action.

The Ramadi deployment did not require more than just showing up at the blow-up scene. US medics helped clean up the carnage, and two days later, the 7th was on its way back to the Green Zone, after the Sunnis assured everyone they could handle the situation. Maliki swore his Shi'ite troops knew nothing about the slaughter, although the Sunnis suspected it.

On the relaxed trip back to Baghdad, Bis and Tooley were, at last, given a bit of deployment respite, and used it to talk about the deteriorating Iraq situation.

Bis complained to Tooley, "As we both know, our Strykers, and, in fact, all of the GI's in Iraq, are totally dependent on the supply highways which run along both the Tigris River and the Euphrates River, all coming from our supply ships landing in Kuwait, and also from the other ports on the Persian Gulf."

"I'm fully aware of the continuing long and slender lines of US supply trucks, which each day move stuff to our troops," Tooley responded.

"Any widespread terrorist guerilla actions, either Sunni, or Shi'ite, or both, could easily disrupt, slow, or even fully stop those trucks from getting the job done," Bis commented.

"The Brigade First Sergeant told me, at least five hundred tanker trucks a day, are needed just to provide fuel for American combat vehicles, let alone those necessary for the rest of the supplies," Tooley offered.

"If only half of those trucks were somehow not allowed to get through to our troops," Bis intoned, "and then abetting cooperating terrorists started a general offensive operation, say in Baghdad, or Karbala, American forces, for lack of fuel, would not be able to respond, or not effectively respond."

"I'm sure the diabolical terrorist minds have pondered that very scenario," Tooley added, as their Stryker caravan pulled back into the protective Green Zone fortress.

Bis, Tooley, and his Strykers, looked forward to a few stressless days, sleeping in a bed, and eating some hot chow, but it was not to be.

October 15th found the 7th Squadron deployed, this time, back in Sadr City, patrolling the, now quiet streets, but which eight hours earlier, had bristled with raging warfare, between members of Sadr's reconstituted militia army, and Maliki's security forces, the government's poorly trained and disciplined troops had sustained, in the fight, great losses of men and equipment. While no overt action could be seen now, Bis sensed, and in most cases saw, likely Sadr Shi'ite militia lounging idly around in the areas the Squadron was now patrolling.

"Where do you go? Do you arrest all you see on the street without a reason? What is possible?" Bis asked Tooley.

"We no longer can figure out who is friend, and who is foe," Tooley lamented, adding, "Maliki and his government troops are supposed to be friendly, but they are not. Sadr's Mahdi Army is supposed to be toothless, but they are not."

Bis then responded, saying, "Also Bush and his generals have given our recent Hussein Sunni enemies re-control of Anbar Province, so we have no idea whether we should shoot them, or shoot with them, after Maliki's Shi'ites move in to shoot, or arrest them," adding, "Our GI's are involved and yet they are not involved. If we do get into firefights, will we then be prosecuted by the Iraqi government, or will we be court marshaled by the US Military, if we don't?"

Tooley laughed out loud, "What a complete, mad, Bush/neo-con mess."

"The mess in Afghanistan is also getting messier and messier," Bis pointed out, after directing his Stryker driver to run one more lap around the Squadron's appointed Sadr City patrol route, "That nation is proving so corrupt and ungovernable that it would be better for all if the US just pulled out of there."

"The people that run Afghanistan, whether Karzai government officials, local warlords, Taliban-ites, or bureaucrats, they are all corrupt," Tooley commented, "Between them, they have forced the poor Afghan people into a state of opium drug addiction, while at the same time, collecting high profits from these same people."

As the 7th Squadron finished its appointed patrol run, Bis then told his driver to head back to the Green Zone. After that, Bis responded to Tooley's comment, saying, "While we can all feel sympathy for the Afghan people, they have been treated in a similar manner for hundreds of years by the same-same political leaders. My concern has to be for the American Marines remaining in Afghanistan. They, like us in Iraq, are dependent for all their supplies on the endless convoys of trucks that trek the twelve hundred miles from Karachi on the Arabian Sea, to Peshawar and the Khyber Pass, in order to reach Kabul in Afghanistan. Oil, fuel, food, heavy equipment, hospital supplies, and other necessary items, are trucked in, at a cost of several million dollars a day," chuckling as he then added, "You wouldn't believe that America assumes another one million a day, in Pakistan road tolls."

Tooley looked quizzically at Bis, and intoned, "You don't mean it. Our good ally, Pakistan, to whom we have freely given billions of dollars, charges our supply trucks a road toll. Now that is gratitude."

"A few days ago, threatened with Pakistan road closures, the Bush Administration cut a check to Pakistan's new president, Asif Zardari, supposedly for one year's worth of tolls, or totaling three hundred sixty-five million American taxpayer bucks, in order to keep American trucks on their lousy, rutted roads, competing with donkey carts, camel drawn wagons, and bicycles," adding, "The point is, our troops there can be put in dire circumstances, by merely cutting off our supplies and for any reason. What do you do? How do you fix it? We really cannot trust in any Islamic institution."

Tooley, nodding in agreement, pointed out, "Even some American media are saying that Karzai's Afghan government's corruption and his lack of accountability are contributing to the Taliban resurgence, and the billions in aid has been thrown out the window," adding, "Karzai refuses to address the poppy cultivation problem, and, as such, no matter what the US does, it cannot cure the problem."

"If you are asking where the money goes," Bis interpled, "look no farther than to the top Karzai government officials with exaggerated salaries, the prime Afghan contractors, the sub-contractors on the various American backed projects, and to all the other Afghan's dipping into the pot," laughing at the thought.

The 7th Stryker Squadron, collectively, experienced great relief, as its vehicle returned back through the front gate of the Green Zone, and they moved back into their welcoming barracks.

But this, again, was not to be a lingering rest, which the Squad had enjoyed only a few weeks before.

By the following Monday, October 20, 2008, the whole 711th Stryker Brigade, was ordered deployed to patrol the Shi'ite held Diyala Province area, a few miles northeast of Baghdad, where, a few hours earlier, Sunni insurgents had attacked a gathering of Shi'ite police officers, at the home of the Shi'ite local police commissioner. They were celebrating his release from an earlier detention by the US Command for cooperating with members of Sadr's Mahdi Army.

Bis was now overwhelmed with great concern when confronted by these continuing happenings in Iraq, and the obvious long-term danger to the Stryker Brigade, plus the complete disregard of these significant facts by the Bush/neo-cons and their kept American generals.

The 711th Squadron was assigned the patrol area near Balad Ruz, the Diyala Province city where the insurgent attacks occurred, causing the death of thirty Sadr Shi'ites, and the wounding of many more.

Bis commented to Tooley, as they motored around their sector, "This area was viciously taken over by Saddam Hussein, and, at the time, became predominantly Sunni controlled. Maliki is trying to stack it with his brand of Shi'ite. This plan has obviously failed, and even though Bush and Maliki are delighted to see the Sadr forces meet their fate, it seems obvious to me, that our former Sunni enemies now completely surround the 711th Stryker Brigade, and all other Iraqi US Forces, as they peacefully drink coffee in Baghdad. They are in complete control in Anbar, and now seem capable of re-assuming control in critical parts of Diyala."

Tooley nodded in assent, offering, "We could be setting up American Forces in the Baghdad area for a big surprise," adding, "Promoting control by a former enemy, and then supplying him with American arms is not a very rational policy."

"Bush and his neo-con handlers never even considered the fact that the Emir controlled people in Iraq have never, in all their history, known a so-called Western-type democracy. The Sunni are brainlessly called upon, and the Shi'ite are also called upon, by the neo-cons, to put complete trust and cooperation in each other, when all each has ever known, is certain death from the other. Iraqis are told that previous Sunni or Shi'ite patronage and privilege would have to move over to a so-called free market, controlled by foreign interests. Further that their ancient beliefs regarding the status of men as to women would now have to be modified," adding, "It obviously is impossible and only serves to rile both Sunni and Shi'ite against the occupying American."

The driver of Bis' Stryker suddenly braked to a complete stop, saying, "Trouble ahead."

Bis looked out his peek hole, and saw, standing in the street, Iraqi government uniformed security forces congregated in the city square. He watched as a small group moved to one side, and began yelling. "Allah is great. Allah is good. Mohammad is his messenger," and then discharged their American supplied Colt carbines into the air.

Ordering his 7th Squadron to stay in their vehicle, and ending with a warning, "That is an order, men. I have a necessary job I need to do. What I have to say, would not be approved by the officers."

With that, Bis climbed up out of the Stryker, through its top hatch. He then stood straight and tall, and proclaimed, in as loud a voice as he could muster, "God is great. God is good. God is love.

God is everything. Jesus Christ, His son, is His only messenger."

Whether the Iraqi's understood was doubted, but the 7th Squadron did, and cheered and cheered, as Bis returned back into the now-re-rolling Stryker.

Chapter XXV –
The Over Current

Bis and his Squadron did manage to get a few days of rest and relaxation following the last deployment.

On Thursday, October 23, 2008, Bis and Tooley were even able to get in a couple of Gin Rummy card games at the NCO Mess following lunch.

Tooley laughingly accused Bis of pulling cards out of no where, when, time after time, Bis found the card key to call "Gin", telling his Corporal, "It's the living of a good, honest, Christian life. It not only wins at cards, but also wins at life," chuckling.

During one of the shuffles, Tooley asked Bis if he had ever heard of the "March 14th Movement".

Bis responded shaking his head no, after which Tooley replied, "The Brigade First Sergeant says it is also part of the Shi'ite-Sunni fight. This time it is in Lebanon. It seems the Saudi Arabian Sunni royalty is laying down a lot of money in Lebanon to counter the Shi'ite-Hezbollah coup where, under a so-called

'Qatar Peace Agreement', Hezbollah was given veto power over any action of Lebanon's government it does not like, along with a legal right to keep their weapons, and to form a militia. The First Sergeant insists that what Saudi's are doing is trying to cultivate a Sunni-Wahhabi ideology in Lebanon."

Wahhabism I know," Bis responded. "It is the most violent form of Islam. It was the motivation of those who flew into the Trade Towers on 9-11. It is what Saudis are trying to introduce in American schools and Mosques. It is the most anti-Christian of all the Moslem teachings, a real danger to the West.

Tooley, finding the cards finally moving his way, shouted, "Gin," and, as Bis was putting the count down on paper, he continued, saying, "That is interesting, because the reason the Brigade First Sergeant was interested is that Representative Gary Ackerman, the Democrat Chairman of the House Foreign Affairs Subcommittee on the Middle East, wanted information from the Brigade. Ackerman has, evidently, severely criticized the Bush Administration for failing to do more to provide backing for this 'March 14th Sunni Alliance'," adding, "I guess the 'March 14th' name was taken from the assassination of a Lebanese Prime Minister on that Date. My point is the Sunni-Shi'ite tit for tat is everywhere in the Middle East."

"A point well taken," Bis admitted. "I think the Sunni problem is worse than the Shi'ite problem, Sadr and all," adding, "And speaking of points, I just went out. You owe me twenty dollars."

Bis continued, "I'm surprised Ackerman is supporting the Sunni side. The Sunni's don't love

Israel, as much as the Shi'ites don't love Israel," chuckling, "I guess the reason is Iran is Shi'ite. Israel would be better off staying out of Lebanese politics, and instead make a deal directly with Iran. They are going to get stung again, just as they did in their recent losing war in Lebanon."

Tooley reached into his pocket and began counting out twenty dollars, and as he did, one of the Squadsmen of the 7th came rushing in and informed Bis that the Squadron had received new orders to deploy, along with the 3rd Stryker Squadron, and the 5th Stryker Squadron, on the following morning, October 24th. Bis and Tooley, surprised by the announcement, hurried back to their barracks to get more particulars on this very troublesome deployment.

Bis and the Squadron had been informed of the details by the Brigade Regimental Commander's newly delivered, written orders. They outlined details that new fighting had occurred between the Sunni "Sons of Iraq", which are the American paid Sunni security forces in Anbar Province, and the Shi'ite government security forces sent into the Anbar Province city of Fallujah, to arrest supposed Sunni terrorists, by Maliki. The three Squadrons were ordered to deploy to Fallujah, starting at 0600 hours on October 24th. They were also instructed to take a tanker fuel truck, and supply trucks with rations and supplies for three days. They were further ordered to keep in radio contact with the Regiment every four hours, to report any progress or problems.

As Bis and Tooley then gathered in Bis' room to contemplate these regimental orders, and to prepare for the deployment the following morning, Bis commented, "I thought something like this would happen. A few days ago, Maliki's government, under Bush-Odierno's urging, began to assume authority over, and to integrate into the Maliki government, the tens of thousands of Sunni, 'Sons of Iraq', fighters scattered around, not only Anbar Province, but also Ninewa, Diyala, and Salah ad Din Provinces. These are former, dangerous, Sunni strongholds, and if Maliki and his Shi'ites think they can assume control of these guys without a fight, even with American backing, they are badly mistaken. So are Bush and General O'Dierno. They can't seem to get it out of their heads that everybody should be nice to one another, because they say so," adding, "It was a stupid, risky, Bush policy to re-arm, and then to pay these former Sunni enemy fighters. They were hired to chase al-Qaeda, but any al-Qaeda presence is merely a mirage. The Sunnis' real enemy is the Shi'ite, just as the Shi'ites' real enemy is the Sunni."

"It is a testy, volatile, situation," Tooley agreed, and then began rolling over in his mind the supplies they would need for three days in the field.

"It is hard to figure out what to do," Bis admitted. "I would not like to be our Regimental Commander. He gets orders to rely on the US paid Anbar Sunni troops, so-called allies, and also, at the same time to rely on Maliki's Shi'ite government security forces," adding, "It is an impossibility. One faction, one way, or another, is going to dominate over the other."

"And usually by violence," Tooley intoned, adding, "To give them such free wheeling is only putting the US Troops in big danger."

Tooley continued, "Secretary Gates tells us, 'Don't worry,' he will deploy six, three thousand five hundred each, strong, US army brigades to Iraq, but this, like the three combat brigades, which are supposed to go to Afghanistan, are slated for next summer, not now. American troop strength is now down to one hundred twenty-five thousand people, with only fifty percent of them having any combat experience."

"Every place we have been sent in the last two months," Bis acknowledged, "has been because of Sunni against Shi'ite violence," adding, "It has usually been Shi'ite beating up on Sunni 'Sons of Iraq', but I think the Sunni worm is going to turn, in Anbar, Diyala, Tamin, and Salah ad Din Provinces. They are Sunni dominated provinces. In pre-Iraq War time, they formed Saddam Hussein's base. If you look closely at a map, it is also obvious that these provinces completely surround Baghdad, including the Green Zone."

"They also control all the road networks south to Basra, and those east to Jordan and Lebanon," Tooley murmured.

The 7th Squadron got off, in good shape, and on time, at 0600 hours, the following morning, Friday, October 24, 2008.

As their Stryker caravan formed up, moving east from Baghdad on the way to Fallujah, the 7th Stryker was put in the lead, on point, followed by the 5th Stryker, where the officers in command, and communications were stationed, and then came the, several hundred gallon fuel tanker, and the two supply trucks, followed up, in the rear, by the 3rd Stryker Squadron.

The several mile trip to the Sunni city gave Bis and Tooley time to discuss their situation.

When they came to the first major road intersection in Anbar, just past the Tigris, Tooley pointed out, "That is the main road to Kirkuk and Mosul. We want to keep that in mind. It might be handy."

Bis then interpled, "There is another improved road, several miles east, past Ramadi, which cuts back to both cities."

"Speaking of Kurdistan, did you see where the Kurd president, Jalal Talabani, approved the recently enacted Iraqi law which sets provincial elections for members of Iraq's Parliament. They say elections will beheld prior to January 31, 2009," Tooley commented.

"The approval, however, comes with some very important exceptions," Bis replied. "First of all, they took out the provision which would have divided Kirkuk's oil equally between Shi'ites, Sunnis, and Kurds. Secondly, they removed an Article which would have guaranteed Christians a certain number of seats in the next Parliament."

"The Christians always are considered last, if at all," Tooley lamented, adding, "Both the Sunnis and Muqtada al-Sadr's Shi'ites are hoping to make big gains in the election. Looks like the Kurds will still maintain their virtual sovereignty no matter what."

"That's a given," Bis responded, adding, "We better stop talking and start keeping a close eye. We are now only a few miles from Fallujah. The Captain ordered each Stryker Squad to maintain one hundred yards distance between us," as he checked out his peephole, and finding they were too close, directed his driver to speed up, in order to spread the units an additional twenty-five yards.

"Did you notice all the Iraqi males lounging around the main streets, as we passed through those last two villages?" Tooley commented.

Bis nodded yes, and then turned, telling his Squad, "We don't know what we will come across up ahead. Check you rifles. Put in a clip, and then keep them at the ready, and set on safety."

The caravan, by now, had just entered the outskirts of Fallujah. As it slowed down, and headed for the center of town, Bis could hear the Captain talking over the radio, with an interpreter, trying to contact the Iraq Sunni authorities at the City Hall.

All at once, there was a blinding, gigantic, huge explosion. It was so extensive that it lifted the rear end of the 7th Stryker vehicle, even with its several thousands of pounds weight, plus nine Squadsmen inside, a few inches off the pavement.

"Wow," Tooley shouted. "What was that?"

Bis, getting the lay of this hostile land out of his armored peephole, and windshield, ordered his driver to speed up, in order to waylay any ambush intended for their Stryker.

When no further blowups occurred, Bis then directed his driver to make a U-turn. He tried to make contact with the communications, and his officers, in the 5th Squadron Stryker and heard no response.

Bis, finally was able to make radio contact with the sergeant in command of the 3rd Stryker.

"You would not believe what I saw," the Sergeant screamed. "The 5th Stryker vehicle just disappeared. All that's left is a big hole in the pavement," adding, "There are also terrorists behind us, moving in on our position."

"What about the tanker and the two trucks?" Bis asked.

"While we were going into Fallujah, the slow tanker and trucks fell behind, pushing us behind by several yards," the Sergeant responded. "That saved them and us."

"Can you get past the IED damage?" Bis asked. "Is there anything we can do to help the 5th?"

"They just don't exist anymore," the Sergeant replied, adding, "It looks like we can make it around the hole."

"It would be disastrous to try to go back to Baghdad now." Bis yelled into his radio. You better bring the tanker and trucks, and your Stryker through, and we will make a run for Ramadi. We should be able to get help there, and also make contact with Baghdad."

"They must have used all the explosives in Iraq," the Sergeant hollered, "to make a hole like that. They also must have triggered it by remote control. Our good luck, the Fifth's bad luck."

The Sergeant continued, after a short break, saying, "We made it through. We should be with you in a minute," adding, "Sergeant Bismarck, since we have no remaining officers, as far as I'm concerned, you are in command."

It was only a brief trip to Ramadi for Bis' shortened convoy, and as they entered the city, it was ominously eerie.

Sensing danger, Bis contacted the 3rd Stryker Sergeant, warning, "I don't like it. It's too quiet," adding, "Double your speed, and if we are fired upon, make a bee-line for the outskirts of the city, and keep moving. There is a major intersection thirty miles on, where we can stop and talk, and fuel up.

Rifles began to be heard popping as the two Strykers and their trucks moved to the center of Ramadi. The rifle pings increased the farther in they moved. The increased speed, however, got them through unscathed, and they then quickly covered the thirty miles to the big intersection.

Bis, on the way, kept trying to contact Baghdad, but could not raise anyone. Tooley, seeing his dilemma, volunteered his help, saying, "I think I can get through to the Brigade First Sergeant. He has his own personalized radio, and I know the frequency. Let me try."

Bis gladly moved over so Tooley could fiddle with the radio knobs, and as he was trying to find the right radio frequency, Tooley commented, "Did you see what kind of arms the terrorists were using to shoot at us?"

"I thought I saw American Colt rifles," Bis responded. "Just like we carry."

"That's what I saw," Tooley replied, suddenly straightening up, saying, "I think I got the First Sergeant," and began talking into the receiver, starting by indentifying himself.

"I thought that was you, Tooley," a weak voice broke through the static. I knew you guys were deployed to Fallujah. What happened? What's going on?"

He continued, "All hell has broken loose here. The rest of the Brigade is scattered around defending various parts of Baghdad. We are under attack from terrorists from Tamin and Salah ad Din, along with Diyala Provinces. We have not really identified the insurgents yet, but Maliki's security force, which was thrown into the fray, deserted as quickly as they hit the ground. What is going on in Anbar?"

Tooley explained what happened, and that they lost the 5th Stryker, and their officers. Further, that wherever they moved in Anbar, they were under attack."

Tooley then handed the receiver to Bis, and as he did so, told the Brigade First Sergeant, "I'm putting Sergeant Bismarck on. He is the Senior Sergeant and in command. He will explain our dilemma."

"Hello Sergeant. Thank God we have been able to contact someone in Baghdad."

"Hi Sergeant Bismarck. I will inform the Brigade Command about your problems in Anbar Province. What are you going to do now?"

"We are at the main intersection east of Ramadi. We will fuel up, and head north to Kirkuk or Mosul," adding, "We will contact you tomorrow for any further orders."

"I want to warn you, Sergeant," the Brigade First Sergeant responded, "We are getting reports from the southern US commands in Nasiriyah, and Basra, that elements of Sadr's militia have closed off all the supply roads leading to Baghdad, and we in Baghdad could be having fuel problems for all of our combat vehicles unless the problem is solved quickly," adding, "Good luck. I will keep this frequency open for you."

The radio then went dead, and deadly quiet reigned in the Bismarck convoy.

"It could be worse," Bis commented, laughing, "We could have tried to make it back to Baghdad."

CHAPTER XXVI –
THE FLIGHT TO SANITY

It was developing into a lightless landscape on that fateful October 24th, as Bis and his Stryker caravan sped northwest on the only road open to them, which, if followed to its end, would bring them to Kirkuk.

As it got more dark, Bis ordered a stop to talk things over, and also to stretch and relax.

Military "C" rations were passed around, which filled his troops with much needed nutrition, and the energy to move on.

Bis, after the stop, told all his anxious, assembled men, "We are about ten miles from the Tigris River. Its then about another fifty miles to Kirkuk. The Kurds control part of Kirkuk, but there are a lot of Arab Sunnis in the city, and I don't trust them right now, especially since we will be coming into the city in complete darkness, and they don't know we are coming."

"Do we have any other choice?" the Sergeant from the 3rd Squadron asked.

"Just before we get to the Tigris, there is a good paved road going north, following the Tigris, to Mosul, a city which is mostly Kurd," Bis replied. "Its about seventy-five miles to Mosul, but about twenty-five miles south of Mosul is a small village called Tel Asquf."

"I remember that name," Tooley interjected. "That is the village where many of the Chaldean Christians fled to when their Arch Bishop, Paulos Faraj Rabho, was kidnapped and killed in Mosul," shaking his head, adding, "Sounds like Mosul can also be a problem for Americans."

Bis nodded, and commented, "The town of Tel Asquf has a few thousand residents, and most of them are Iraqi Christians," adding, "I understand that the village, by agreement with the Kurds, is protected by an all Christian militia. The Kurds even armed them with Kalashnikov automatic rifles. They must have had a surplus."

"That's a good sign," Tooley admitted.

As Bis stood to show his fellow squadsmen a map, the tanker driver suddenly walked up to the group announcing, "All the vehicles are tanked up, and I still have more than half left."

As Bis nodded, the 3rd Squadron Sergeant interposed, "Its nice to have your own mobile gas station," laughing, "Whoever decided on including the tanker in our caravan was right on."

"Good job," Bis commented, and then informed his troops, "Look, I don't know what to expect. I think we should go to the Tigris, and then stop and talk it over again. Between here and the river, go no faster than thirty miles per hour, and each Stryker post a man on top with the heavy guns, if we should run into any opposition."

The trip to the river was uneventful, even though it was completely dark. The road remained mostly good, and mostly empty. Donkey carts usually found, so not operate at night.

When the Tigris was reached, Bis' Stryker in the lead, pulled over to the side of the road and after posting guards, and scouting out the immediate area, made his decision.

"Its midnight. To try to get to Kirkuk would be too dangerous, and we are not sure of our reception."

Bis continued, "We head north to Tel Asquf. Its about fifty miles to Mosul, so I judge the village at twenty-five to thirty miles."

Tooley nodded in agreement and the 3rd Stryker Sergeant replied, "I agree. That is our best and safest bet."

"I am going to be riding up front in one of the trucks with the 7th Stryker trailing behind me, and the 3rd bringing up the rear," Bis declared. "I want three hundred yards between the truck and the Stryker. I don't want to scare the Christians, but I want to make sure we protect our guys," adding, "We will proceed at only twenty-five miles per hour, so it could be two or three hours before we are in the vicinity of Tel Asquf. Make sure you Strykers keep a gunner on top, and I want two guys from the 7th armed, riding in back of my truck, and two guys from the 3rd armed, riding in the second truck."

"Anything else?" the 3rd Sergeant asked.

"We don't know what to expect, so half of you keep an eagle eye, and half get a few hours of sleep," Bis responded.

Again the trip, even at such a slow pace, was uneventful, and it was 0300 hours when the driver of Bis' truck nudged him, as Bis had nodded off, saying, "Sergeant, there is a light ahead. I thought you had better check it out."

"Thanks," Bis responded, and got out of his truck and then walked back to both Strykers.

"That light has to be connected to Tel Asquf," Bis told them. "I'm going to take my truck slowly forward with my lights blinking. You remain here. Put out perimeter guards, and wait for my signal."

Bis directed his somewhat reluctant driver to move slowly forward the approximate two blocks to the light ahead. As they got closer, they came across a sand barrier, which seemed to extend, like a snake, off both sides of the highway. At that point, a voice ahead yelled, in the Iraqi, and then, also, in the Kurdish dialect, "Halt. Get out of your vehicle and walk slowly to this checkpoint."

Bis cautioned his driver to keep the motor going, and to wait for him.

"Should you do this?" the driver asked. "You don't know what to expect."

"I don't have any other choice," Bis responded, getting out of the truck. "I'll be back shortly, I hope."

As Bis walked up to the closed barricade, the voice yelled, "I can see you are dressed in an American uniform. Are you an American crusader? What are you doing here?"

Bis raised his arms over his head, and asked, "Do you speak English?"

"Wait," was the answer.

Fully two minutes later another voice, this time in English, called out, "Move forward. Keep your arms up."

Bis complied, and walked the few remaining yards, but still was not able to see, as they kept a strong searchlight focused on his face.

The light was covered, and Bis was finally able to recognize forms and people, in their almost total darkness.

Bis set forth, and in a loud voice stated, "My name is Sergeant Bismarck. We are stationed in Baghdad. We are here because we are unable to get back to our base. Do you have an American command here?"

"I am sure the Americans in Baghdad are having big problems according to my radio reports," the Iraqi man exclaimed, for the first time coming into Bis' view. "My name is Samoon Petrus. I am one of the elected Christian militia leaders."

He then stepped forward and shook Bis' extended hand, saying, "I will shake hands with American Sergeants. I will not shake hands with American officers. I don't trust them."

"What does your radio say about Baghdad?" Bis asked.

"It says you are running out of gas," the militia leader responded. Insurgents around Nasiriyah, evidently, have cut off your fuel supply line, and the American command in Baghdad's Green Zone doesn't have enough fuel to send their combat machines out to patrol and control the area," adding, "You have a real problem. How did you get enough gas to get here?"

Bis ignored the question, with one of his own, asking, "Is this Tel Asquf?"

"It is," answered Samoon. "Usually anyone not from here is banned. This is a Kurd protected Christian enclave," adding, "We have had enough of both Sunni and Shi'ite terrorists trying to kill us. There are four entrances to this city, and we have Christian armed militia guards at all points."

"We are on our way to Mosul," Bis declared, "But if it is possible, we would like to rest here 'til daylight."

"My friend," Samoon replied, "That is not only possible, but wise. I don't think I would go into Mosul in the dark, and unannounced," adding, "While we appreciate our Kurdish hosts, who are our protectors, we did lose our Arch Bishop Paulos Rabho, who was killed by Islamic terrorists in Mosul just a few months ago."

"I heard about that," Bis lamented. "I'm sorry."

"Since you Americans came to Iraq," Samoon interposed, "Christians have become the ready targets of all Arab Muslims," adding, "Most of us Christians are Chaldean, and our ancestors go back to the time of Christ. At one time, we were almost a million strong in Iraq, but the killings have cut us in half. I once had a store in Baghdad before I was forced to flee to Tel Asquf."

Bis nodded in sympathy, and then asked, "I notice you have a voice projector. Can I use it to tell my people to come forward? That it is okay."

Samoon nodded yes, and then told his fellow militiaman, in Kurdish, to begin blinking his search light. The voice projector, and the blinking light, did the trick, as Tooley slowly brought the caravan toward the checkpoint.

"Don't be surprised to see our gunners on top of our battle Strykers," Bis warned. "I will walk toward them, and reassure them that everything is alright."

"So you are driving the magnificent Strykers," Samoon replied. "I have heard about them."

"You don't provide the only protection to Tel Asquf, do you?" Bis commented.

"If you had gone five miles further," Samoon replied, "You would have been stopped, or worse, by the Kurdistan National Army. The Kurds, or Peshmerga, as the Kurdish Army is called, control all the roads leading to Mosul," adding, "It is the Peshmerga who provided my two hundred militiamen with our Kalashnikov rifles, and who give us each two hundred dollars per month to protect this village."

"Do the Sunnis still give you any trouble?" Bis asked, as he moved out from the barricade, toward the approaching caravan.

"Not any more," Samoon responded. "The Arab Sunnis don't try to buck the Peshmerga. They have been beat up too many times. The Kurds run this area, and they know it."

Bis moved out, holding up his hand to stop the caravan about a half block from the barricade. At that point, he called out to Tooley and to the 3rd Sergeant, and told them, "It looks like we have a safe haven, at least for now."

"Everything okay?" Tooley asked.

"Come on. I want you to meet the Christian boss of the Christian town of eight thousand souls," Bis responded.

As the three walked toward the barricade, Bis explained the appearance of Samoon, and his gracious offer of protection.

"It is now almost 0500, Tooley," Bis explained. "I want you to get on and stay on our radio. See if you can raise your Brigade Sergeant. We have to find out what the situation is in Baghdad."

Samoon interjected, saying, "It does not look good. The Americans depend on machines. The machines depend on gas. The officers can't deploy the troops to stop the terrorists because they don't have the gas to go after them. The Americans also don't have any convenient available troops from the US to deploy," laughing, "It is what you call a 'Catch 13'."

Bis nodding, told Tooley, "Stay on the radio. We have to know the situation."

"Now I know how you got here," Samoon intoned, laughing, "I see you brought your own gas station," adding, "Sergeant Bismarck, pull your machines and your people over behind that sand barricade for now," pointing, "We will have to talk further in the daylight when we have further information."

At 0800 hours, Tooley was finally able to rouse the Brigade First Sergeant.

"What's going on in Baghdad?" Tooley asked, after identifying himself.

"You are lucky you got through to me," the First Sergeant responded. "You would not believe what's going on around here. We are completely immobilized because we are out of gas. The Sadr Shi'ites, who have blocked our fuel tankers at Nasiriyah, are aware that we don't have enough GI's to blast them out of the way. The Air Force is dropping plenty of missiles and bombs, but the Sadr militia just digs in, and the only thing that blows up is Iraqi sand and rock, and there is nothing more worthless."

Tooley immediately sent a 7th Squadsman to retrieve Bis as soon as he made contact, and Bis, napping on the shady side of the Stryker, soon appeared.

Handing the radio to Bis, Tooley commented, "It's the First Sergeant. Things don't look so good."

"Hi, Sergeant Bismarck here," Bis interposed. "I understand you have fuel problems. What is the Maliki government doing to assist you?"

"His troops defect to Sadr as soon as they are deployed," the Brigade Sergeant replied. "But the Brigade's biggest worry is the Sunnis. They have been armed by Petraeus, and now are in control of Diyala and Salah ah Din Provinces, and most of Anbar," adding, "A big problem is that Maliki has announced he is taking command and control of fifty-four thousand Sons of Iraq Sunni fighters, scattered through those Sunni Provinces. They were formerly supervised and paid, for the last two years, by Petraeus. Maliki claims he will begin paying them in November."

"That could be a real problem," Bis agreed.

"The Sunnis don't believe Maliki," the Brigade Sergeant intoned, "and they are now blaming the Americans for betraying them by allowing Maliki to try to take control. They feel cheated, and most of them think that this will allow the government to target, arrest, and kill the Sunnis. The pot is really boiling and could blow up in a real humdinger, with our American GI's in between."

"What about us?" Bis asked. "Can we get back to the Green Zone?"

"Not now," the Brigade Sergeant responded. "Stay where you are. I will tell the commander I have been in contact with you, and that you want instructions," adding, "Contact me at 1100 hours."

Bis, Tooley, and the other squadsmen tried to relax, napping in the shade of their vehicles. It was a different feeling to be guarded over by the ever ready Christian militia, but welcomed.

About ten o'clock, Samoon appeared back on the scene, and reported directly to Bis, saying, "The militia contacted the Peshmerga about your presence, which they already knew about. They agreed that you can stay for now," adding, "They think there is going to be a long term problem between Mosul, Kirkuk, and Baghdad, and they don't believe you can get back there without a big, big fight."

"We can't stay here too long either," Bis commented. "We would put both you and us at risk."

Samoon nodded, agreeing, and then pointed out, "There are several United States cargo planes that fly into the Mosul Airport each week bringing preconditioned American aid to Kurdistan. They initiate their flights in Germany, and re-fuel them at a US base in Turkey. If things get out of control, that might be a way for you and your troops, at least temporarily, to get reorganized," adding, "I think I could talk the Kurds into that solution."

"What about our Strykers? What about our equipment?" Bis interposed.

"I think we can keep them out of the hands of the Kurds," Samoon replied, "but only if we put them to use, by our militia guarding Tel Asquf," adding, "I won't deny," laughing, "that I would look forward to operating such a machine. We would keep them in the village."

"If I were to turn our Strykers over to anyone," Bis responded, "It would be to you Christians, but that is not likely. We have to do all we can to get back to Baghdad."

"I understand," Samoon replied. "I know you expect to contact Baghdad at eleven o'clock. Can I listen in? It would be a chance to see inside one of your Strykers," laughing.

"Precisely at eleven o'clock, Bis and Samoon were anxiously waiting as Tooley made the knob adjustments necessary to the Brigade First Sergeant.

"Tooley here," the Corporal declared. "I hope you have good news."

"Not any," the Brigade First Sergeant stated. "Where are you guys anyway?" Are you in Mosul?"

"We are about twenty-five miles south of Mosul in a Christian village called Tel Asquf," Tooley replied.

"Good," the Sergeant responded. "Stay there. Things are deteriorating here. We are not able to find the fuel to mount a counter-attack against the terrorists," adding, "The commander thinks they are Sadr Shi'ites and also Sunnis, and they are now beginning to fight each other. Things have completely shut down in Baghdad."

"What do you want us to do?" asked Tooley.

"The Brigade Commander knows now where you are," the Sergeant answered. "He has got a whole bunch of things on his mind. The State Department and other government agencies are already evacuating, by air, their civilians," adding, "Look, it sounds like you got a good spot. Stay there. You will not be able to contact me for a few days. I will make it a point to be by my radio on Tuesday, October 28th at 1100 hours. Good luck."

"It doesn't sound good," Samoon intoned. "Poor planning," adding, "You should be okay here 'til then. You are lucky you are not in Mosul. The Arab Sunnis have been conducting a Christian witch hunt in Mosul. Several Christians have been murdered, and fifty new Christians have fled here in the past two days."

"Isn't that unusual?" Bis responded. "Usually Kurdistan is more tolerant of Christians."

"These are Arab Islamic killers," Samoon interpled. "It has more to do with Christians in the area lobbying for some set aside seats in the Iraq Parliament."

"We really appreciate your putting us up for a few days," Bis responded, changing the subject. "We really don't have anyplace else to go."

"If you want," Samoon intoned, "Several Christian families have volunteered to have your troopers live with them for a few days. It would be a good time to get some rest in a bed, and to get off of "C" rations."

The next few days were Eden-ish for the Strykers. The radio told of the increasing American problems in Baghdad, but the squadsmen, ironically, were living the good life. October 28th came up too quickly as Bis and Samoon gathered again in the Stryker while Tooley tried to contact Brigade.

The prevailing static, and the other noises, suddenly stopped, as the clear voice of the Brigade First Sergeant came over the radio.

"I wish I were there with you," he declared. "You would not believe how bad it is here. Bush is blaming the generals. The generals are blaming the Pentagon. The Pentagon is blaming Congress. McCain is blaming Obama, and Obama is blaming McCain," adding, "Things have gone downhill fast. Sunnis again are fighting Shi'ite, and terrorists have total control of Baghdad. No possibility exists of a current big troop or fuel surge coming from Basra to our aid. They are just not available. We are on the verge of a total withdrawal of our remaining forces by air and the abandonment of the Green Zone."

Bis, highly concerned, took the radio receiver and asked, "What is the Maliki government doing? Can't they protect you?"

"Any so-called Iraqi security troops are now Sadr Militia," the Brigade Sergeant replied. "Maliki can't even defend his own enclave. Its as though we never came here, except we did, and as a result, a few million Iraqis are now dead, and America has lost five thousand of its finest dead, and fifty thousand GI's are maimed for life. America's military is ruined, and it broke our treasury."

"What about the Allied Forces in the south?" Bis asked.

"They are having a tough time just trying to figure out which end of a rifle shoots, let alone defend us," adding, "The Brigade Commander said to tell you that Baghdad cannot save you. You are to make what agreement you can with the Kurds, and try to make your way, some way, out of Mosul. You are free to use your own judgment in whatever you do. I am not going to be able to contact you again, so good luck."

As the three sat there stunned, the radio static and other noises resumed.

A good three minutes passed in silence before Tooley stated, "Looks like the handwriting is on the wall. At least, he gave Bis the authority to use his own judgment."

Another two minutes elapsed before Bis, putting his hand on Samoon's shoulder, asked, "Do you think you can still arrange a ride out of Mosul on those American cargo planes?"

"I think so," Samoon responded. "Let me try. I will probably need until tomorrow morning to confirm anything."

Neither Bis nor Tooley could get much sleep that night. The following morning, at 0700 hours, Samoon was watched as he approached their Stryker. Both were apprehensive.

Bis and Tooley stood, and walked toward Samoon, as the Christian Iraqi suddenly exposed a huge smile, saying, "You are lucky. The Peshmerga has agreed to let you fly out of Mosul's airport on Friday, October 31, 2008, at 0800 hours," adding, "The reason is the Arab Sunnis' campaign against the Christians. They want us to take care of them, and protect them when they emigrate to Tel Asquf, and they don't want you Americans around to add to the problem."

"What a lifesaver you are," Tooley exclaimed.

"What about the Stryker? What did the Peshmerga say about them?" Bis interposed.

"They reluctantly said we could keep them," Samoon responded. "if we keep them in the village and out of sight."

"Neither the Christians, nor the Peshmerga, have the know how, or the electrical replacement units to keep the Strykers operating too long," Bis murmured, "But with half a tanker of fuel, they should be useful to you for a while," adding, "If you give us two of your best men, Tooley and I will train them in how the Stryker operates. We evidently will be here 'til Friday, October 31st."

Samoon nodded and said, "That would be welcome. I don't know if you will ever reclaim your magnificent machines, but if you do, they will be in immaculate condition."

By Thursday evening, Bis and Tooley had shown two Christian designated drivers the intricacies of the Stryker. That evening, the 7th and the 3rd Strykers, also were invited to Christian church services by the village, held in the American's honor, and Bis was offered an opportunity to render a prayer on behalf of all who were effected by the sudden Iraqi crisis.

Bis walked up to the alter and said, "I am going to paraphrase a prayer given by one of my heroes, Aleksandr Solzhenitsyn, which I think is appropriate."

Bis got down on his knees and prayed, saying, "How easy it is to live with you, dear Christ, dear God. How easy to believe in you, when my spirit is overwhelmed within me. When all of us can see no further than the night, and don't know what tomorrow will bring, you make it easy for us to believe that you exist, and are mindful of me, and us, and that the path to righteousness is open."

As Bis then got up from his knees, the congregation burst into an applause of abetting prayer confidence.

The following morning, Friday, at 0400 hours, Bis, the 3rd Sergeant, and Tooley, had everyone but Bis loaded in one of the trucks, front and back.

Bis rode up front of the small caravan in Samoon's American Humvee, which the Iraqi Christian only took out on special occasions.

By 0630 hours, the group had passed through three Kurd checkpoints, and arrived at the gates of the Mosul airport, at which point it stopped, and Samoon, getting out of his Humvee, told the Strykers bunched into the one truck, "I have to leave you now. The

Peshmerga will conduct you directly to the American cargo plane. Don't worry. They can be trusted."

Samoon continued, "I am happy to have met all of you. Tell the Christians in America to take more control over their government. If they don't, they will end up like Europe, which is no longer Christian."

Bis walked to Samoon, and embraced him, saying only one word, "Thanks."

Bis and his Strykers, watched as Samoon departed, under the watchful eye of the Kurdistan guards.

At 0730 hours, the Kurd officer instructed Bis to get into the truck, and then told a Kurd soldier to drive the truck to the American cargo plane sitting off the main runway.

By 0745 hours, the Strykers were boarding the thirty year old, well conditioned American cargo plane. They were greeted by a weathered Major, a pilot holding an unlit cigar in his mouth, who announced, "Welcome to Little America."

At precisely 0800 hours, the plane moved effortlessly, even with all aboard, down the main runway, and into the Kurdistan skies.

Bis made his way forward to the cockpit, as the plane continued, saying to himself as the landscape was now visible, *"Alas poor Iraq, I knew it well,"* paraphrasing Shakespeare.

"Did you say something?" asked the pilot.

"Nothing," Bis responded. "Just talking to myself."

"That is a professional hazard in this business," the pilot responded, adding, "You guys are lucky. They've got lots of trouble in Baghdad."

The pilot continued, "You will be home in time to vote. Are you going to vote for the crooks in Congress, or for the crooks that are running to take Bush, the traitor's job," laughing.

"I'm going to vote for George," Bis related.

"He is not running again, is he?" the pilot chuckled.

"I meant George Washington," Bis corrected, as the pilot and co-pilot, after a few seconds, laughed so loud it could almost be heard in the Kurdistan village below them.